facebook.com

Business Bliss ?

Ignorance: Liability or Bliss

Tobi McNeil, CPIM

iUniverse, Inc.
New York   Bloomington

Business Bliss ?
Ignorance: Liability or Bliss

The views expressed in this work are solely those of the author and do not necessarily reflect the views of the publisher, and the publisher hereby disclaims any responsibility for them.

iUniverse books may be ordered through booksellers or by contacting:

iUniverse
1663 Liberty Drive
Bloomington, IN 47403
www.iuniverse.com
1-800-Authors (1-800-288-4677)

Because of the dynamic nature of the Internet, any Web addresses or links contained in this book may have changed since publication and may no longer be valid.

ISBN: 978-1-4401-2822-6 (pbk)
ISBN: 978-1-4401-2824-0 (cloth)
ISBN: 978-1-4401-2823-3 (ebk)

Library of Congress Control Number: 2009924292

Printed in the United States of America

iUniverse rev. date: 3/11/2009

To my mother,
Irene McNeil

CONTENTS

ACKNOWLEDGEMENTS

Bonnie Bloomquist, my employee and friend has provided me with unmatchable support that every business person dreams about. I could not have done this without her.

Geri Eakins, Linda Kemp, and Arlene Elliott are the most amazing counsellor/coaches on the planet. I will never be able to thank you all enough for showing me how to follow my dreams and get over myself.

I owe deep gratitude to Michelle Nuttall, my wonderful employee. Michelle taught me patience and understanding and I am certain that I learned more from her than she ever did from me.

I would particularly like to thank my sister Sheryn Krywolt for telling me she liked my book at a time when it appeared to be nothing more than personal journaling. I am still unsure how you did it but, you found a way to support me without acting like my big sister.

My mom and dad showed me how to think for myself and how to "go for it" in business. I love you both very much and I miss you dad.

And, I have saved the best for last. I dedicate this book to my loving spouse Greg Karandiuk. Having Greg stand beside through all of my business ventures has given me the strength and confidence to constantly move forward and become a better person. Thank you for being the comic director of this book and my life.

INTRODUCTION

GDK Solutions Inc. is the name of the corporation I created in 2002. The truck manufacturing business that I had worked at for the 5 previous years had just closed their doors and moved to another country. There were plenty of job opportunities available for me but I realized that if I wanted to be the boss, be the one in charge of making decisions, then I needed to open my own company.

To have my own business was a very exciting thought and success was an absolute requirement. I had no intentions of becoming a negative statistic in the abyss of failed business. My research went on for 7 full months until I finally took the plunge and paid my first and last month's rent to the landlord of the building that would house my business center.

Now over 6 years later I look back and realize that I was one of the lucky ones to start a business, run it successfully and sell it for a profit. Lucky because my first year of business was a disaster and I had such a long way to go. My income was almost nonexistent, I was more stressed than I had ever been in my life, I was terrible at training employees, I was doing my own business books, I was taking a beating from existing clients because of my lack of confidence, and my father was diagnosed with terminal cancer,

"Just as I thought things would get no worse, I received a letter from the government advising me that I was about to be audited. If I'd thought I was afraid before, well now I was completely terrified. What was I going to do? How could I get around this? I didn't sleep for one entire week. I was angry, frustrated, and depressed."

Have you ever wondered why some business owners do the right stuff—you know, everything the experts say to do—and still fail; yet on the other hand, another business owner may appear to do everything wrong, and the business becomes a thriving success? The stories in this book are a tiny introduction into the world of small business, including different dilemmas that we all face while trying to juggle our families and our businesses. In today's busy society, there is no specific, cut-and-dried "how to" on opening and running a business.

However, this book is a wonderful and enlightening guide through the ups and downs that many small business owners face before, during, and after they open a small business. My hope is that it will open your eyes to the many variables in life that can affect a small business and help you see the correlation between your business or business ideas and your personal life.

SMALL BUSINESS: TRUST AND INSTINCTS

Often Heard Comment by New Business Owners:
It would be wonderful to open a little business of my own, set my own hours, and make my own decisions.

Reality:
The effort put forth, skills learned, and decisions made in the first year or two of a business can determine whether a business makes it through a third year. It becomes apparent very quickly that running a small business takes time and knowledge—some people find it easy if they have the experience, but most are extremely challenged.

My grandfather, Henry, an extremely healthy man for his entire life, phoned my mother to tell her he was on his way to the hospital, and she had better come. Henry was ninety-six years old when he cleaned up his house (a huge old farm house that he had built himself), drove to the hospital, checked himself in, and prepared to die. I believe he died that evening.

I still shake my head and wonder how he knew what was happening. Then I realized he was doing what he had done all of his life—taking care of himself and trusting his own intuition, as he'd done in business, health, weather, finances, and farming. Henry understood something that we know little about today. He knew what made him comfortable and what didn't feel right.

Henry was likewise intuitive when it came to business. He knew that it was important to plan his business (his farm), and thus, he was able to make it during a time when other businesses were failing. And believe me; others were failing all around him. Henry's business survived the Great Depression, when so many people were forced to walk away from their farms and move to the city to collect subsidies from the government. Henry grew up in a time and place that many of us will never be able to understand. With the help of my grandmother, Johanna, and their six children he farmed, raised cattle and chickens, grew his own vegetables, and built his own house. He couldn't run to the store when he ran out of feed for his livestock because he provided the very food that the animals ate. He did not depend on the things that we take for granted like a corner store, the Internet, online banking, or fast food on every corner. Henry and his family all depended on what he knew and what he sensed, not just what the experts told him. He understood his surroundings and believed in himself, even when others told him he was wrong.

Maybe Henry had fewer outside influences who gave him "expert" advice than we do now, and maybe that somehow made it easier for him to pay attention to his surroundings. His farm was miles away from the neighbors and even farther from the nearest town. His only partner was Johanna who was the glue that helped keep everything in place. She provided positive reassurance to Henry when times were tough and helped him to trust his knowledge about business and farming.

It is really important for all of us to know that the things that made the difference for Henry also apply directly to us today. We need to learn our stuff. What is our stuff? What are our attitudes? How do we become more in tune with our surroundings and believe in ourselves? We need to take the time to quiet our minds and pay attention to our true desires. This doesn't have to take the form of some profound style of meditation; it can simply be sitting in a chair with our eyes closed and breathing deeply for five minutes. There is so much action in our world today that we often forget who we are and what we really think or imagine. Listen to yourself, and you will learn what your true likes and dislikes are. If you are doing something that makes you feel uncomfortable or angry, why are you doing it?

This is the nitty-gritty of why I named this chapter "Small Business: Trust and Instincts." Amazingly, there are thousands of opinions, statistics, and forecasts that claim to know how to open and operate a small business. Unfortunately, this information is based on historical data and generally refers to an average, mythical person opening and growing an average, mythical small business. I often wonder who the average person is because, obviously, I do not fall into that category.

Take the time to know yourself and your business; learn what you can do to put your individual stamp on your work. You are not an "average" person, and it is impossible to compare yourself to a statistic, except for general purposes. You are an individual with your very own special thoughts, which can propel you to greatness.

Many of us today like to follow set patterns that perhaps would guarantee success in our endeavors but there are truly no cut and dried rules on how to operate a successful business. All kinds of things happen that we are not able to plan for and it doesn't matter how much training or planning and forecasting we do, we truly have no way of determining the future.

Forecasts are almost always wrong according to APICS, The Association of for Operations Management[1] and a specific example of this is the terrorist airplanes that took down the World Trade Towers? How many experts knew that the U.S. government would shut down its airspace completely and that the world economy would change overnight? Did anyone predict the sadness and fear that we felt as we watched the news over and over again, wishing that it were all a fictional movie?

We cannot predict the future but we can take responsibility for our reactions to events in our day to day lives. The reactions to these events are what I refer to as "our stuff." We are not average—we are individuals and we all have opportunity to succeed.

Be unique:

- Find a field that you feel passionate about.
- Make your business special.
- Learn from your mistakes
- Learn from mistakes that others have made and do a better job.
- Try a business that is new and exciting.
- Keep moving forward.

If times are hard, do not give in; open your mind to possibilities that you have never thought about:

- Ask other business owners how they might deal with your situation.
- Get advice from long-term businesspeople and decide if it may fit any of your needs.
- Don't be upset if your business doesn't turn out to be exactly what you thought.
- Be adaptable.
- Talk to a professional, certified business coach.

Pointer: Check out existing businesses in the industry and determine what works and what doesn't; then put your special twist on a business of your own.

[1]**Supply Chain Management,** J.R. Tony Arnold, CFPIM, CIRM and Lloyd Clive, CFPIM. APICS - The Educational Society for Resource Management. Falls Church, VA: 1995

YOU HAVE A DREAM

Often Heard Comment by New Business Owners:
I have always dreamed of owning my own little business so I can sit back, relax, and enjoy life.

Reality:
Yes, this does happen—after you work your butt off getting the business up and running, training employees, scrimping and saving, and trying to find ways to pay those ever-so-important employees.

Countless businesses start with only a dream (usually an excellent dream), and the majority of them fail, while some thrive and grow with amazing speed. What is the difference? Why does one business make it and another fail? Dreams are the best place to start and are where many of the best ideas come from. Something most people with ideas don't realize is there are a million ideas out there waiting to be tried. Unless their product is completely unique, it has probably been thought of before. The problem is not the idea; rather, it's the execution of the idea.

The following is a story about a woman named June and how her amazing idea taught her a big life lesson. June decided to open a business selling a product/service that few had ever heard of before. June knew from her research that her product was scientifically based and had amazing results. Employing all her business knowledge, June decided to set up shop. She had a full-time job, with Fridays and weekends off. She thought that three days a week was more than enough time to devote to her business and get it up and running.

She had received permission to sell the product and was ready to start. She found an office for rent and, on the spur of the moment, signed a six-month lease. The office was small, quaint, and affordable, and she purchased just the right furniture, pictures, and decorations, taking great pains to ensure that everything was just right. It was so much fun to start her business; she felt that soon she would be financially free and working her own hours. This was June's perfect solution as she was a newly divorced mother of two teenage boys and wanted to spend lots of quality time with her children.

June had heard that advertising was one of the best ways to get her business known so she went to the newspaper and the radio and spent a great deal of money on advertising. The salespeople she talked to were extremely excited about her idea and assured her she was making the right decision to spend thousands of dollars on an advertising campaign. Their feedback helped to reinforce her decision, and she felt sure it was a good one.

About this time, I suggested she introduce herself to everyone in the building because networking has always been my cheapest and easiest form of advertising. I explained that neighbors are some of the best clients in the world. They would probably refer clients to her if they knew a little about what she did. She told me that she wanted to talk to everyone and would one of these days but that she didn't have time for that right at the moment. Her advertising was starting, and she wanted to be prepared for the influx of calls it would generate. She decided to purchase a land telephone line as she didn't want to tie up her cell phone and run up extremely high bills. She would keep the costs down by utilizing a telephone company with little experience that charged far less than the rest.

It was quite a surprise for June to learn the actual costs of having a business telephone. The telephone company charged over one hundred dollars just to "demark" the telephone line to the electrical closet where she had her office. She also needed an "interconnect" company to connect her phone directly into her office, at a charge of ninety-six dollars per hour. She had never had an account with the telephone company before, and they requested a two hundred fifty dollar deposit to be held for six months—so long as she kept her credit good; if she didn't pay her bills properly they would keep the deposit to cover any outstanding debt. Once the telephone was connected, the costs were approximately forty-five dollars per month, plus long distance charges. Whew! How was that for a really big cost that she had not counted on? She'd spent over five hundred dollars before she even got her first call. Wait, there's more. She hadn't taken into account the tax on her investment, which ended up being about sixty-five dollars.

Someone asked her how she was planning to set up the paperwork side of the business. Should she incorporate? Did she need to buy insurance? Where would she find a good bookkeeper? She told the person that she just didn't have time to sort that portion out, so she would worry about it later.

She knew she would receive money, so she started asking other businesses how they took payments from their clients, and suddenly she was in for another shock. Receipts—what type of receipts would she use? This was the easiest of all her problems, as she could go to the local business supply store and purchase standard receipts. She also realized that some of her clients would pay with cash or by check, but many would use debit and credit cards. It was time to head over to the bank and get that all figured out.

June thought opening a bank account should be easy, and the bank would advise her how to conduct debit and credit card transactions. When she actually met with her bank, the teller immediately asked to see her incorporation documents. Oh no; there was that paperwork problem again. She decided on the spot that she would open a proprietorship because it was easier than incorporating, and the bank would let her open her account virtually immediately. The bank appointment took over two hours because she needed to fill out all the necessary paperwork and do those all-important credit checks. In the meantime, her sons needed rides from school to band practice and she needed to hurry up.

June began to feel the panic rising inside her. All she wanted to do was to get this appointment over with so she could get to her children— she would worry about everything else later. When she arrived, her children were angry because they were late for their practice and they had a mini family feud. June told herself that it was still OK because she was really doing this for her sons so she could be a better parent and spend more time with them.

She was in such a hurry at the bank she'd forgotten to ask about debit and credit card transactions. She was very angry with herself for being so forgetful, which would force her to go back to the bank two days later. Her advertising would be starting in a couple of days, and she needed to be prepared for the many customers she would suddenly have; her forgetfulness was poorly timed (I guess this is a good time to point out that preplanning would have made opening her business much easier, and she probably didn't have to be so hard on herself).

When she finally got back to the bank, June learned the cost involved for a business to own a debit-credit machine, including the monthly charges, plus the percentages that the credit card companies would charge for each transaction. The banker also mentioned that she would need a telephone or a fax line to connect the equipment to; plus there was the issue of where she would keep the machine.

June was suddenly starting to regret the decision to open her own business. She had never been so stressed out before, and most of the money she had set aside to start the business was gone. June decided to use her credit cards; she was sure once the business started making money she would pay them back immediately.

Skip ahead two weeks, and June was extremely depressed. Her advertising had been going for well over a week, and she had only received one phone call to her business line. The most depressing part was the call was from a person who June had connected with on an individual basis and who had not heard any of the advertising. June had still found no time to introduce herself to the people around her, even though she knew they were curious and would probably be interested in her services.

After one full month of advertising, June had still not received a single call and started to think that maybe her dream should have stayed a dream. At this time I suggested again that she walk around the building and introduce herself to the neighboring businesses, but by now she was so depressed that she really didn't feel like introducing herself. Her business wasn't successful, and through her tears, she said she could not understand why. She started to think that perhaps she needed to close her business down.

It had been a full four months since she had come up with her dream to start her business, and June decided that she really wasn't cut out to be a business owner after all. She still had two months left on her office lease and, after that, would probably move the business to her home where it wouldn't cost as much money.

Poor June was not only depressed, she was terribly embarrassed. She had told all her friends, family, and colleagues about her business venture, and now she would have to tell them that she had failed.

But had she really failed? I don't think so, but it does break my heart to know that she set her business up backwards. During the dreaming period, it would have been helpful for June to imagine her business up and running, with clients using and paying for her services. That would have helped her to think through all of her requirements and get her started on a business plan.

A business plan would have helped her determine many of her questions in advance, far before she spent all her start-up money on furniture and advertising. By planning, she would have consulted an accountant and perhaps a lawyer to ensure she was setting up her business in a proper manner. A little research into her potential client base would have taught her that one of the best ways to gain clients is from word of mouth or referrals.

A very important step for June would have been to do some networking with the businesses around her. She would have found that most of the businesses in the neighborhood understood exactly what she was going through and could probably provide helpful advice and even referrals.

The problem with June's setup was that she wanted to do all of the things she found fun and exciting and didn't want to do the necessary groundwork. And when it came down to the nitty-gritty, she didn't have the time. Even though June had done everything she thought would work, she'd failed and wondered why she couldn't gain any customers.

And in her private life, June's sons were driving her nuts—they phoned constantly and made demands on her that she had problems fulfilling. She rushed from her day job to try to get ready for customers and worried about not being there for her children.

The next time June sets up her own business, I suggest that she first make some determinations. These are the questions I recommend that she ask herself:

- Who will be your client base? Will everyone find the product or service useful, or is there only a small percentage who will benefit?

- Ask questions of unbiased parties, such as acquaintances and perhaps, people in related fields. It is quite fun to tell people that you are researching a business and get their response to the idea. But, often our families and close friends, although they mean well, do not give us true feedback because of their own fears.
- Determine whether an advertisement on a popular local radio show would entice potential clients or whether they would follow up on an ad in the local newspaper.
- How important are referrals to this type of business?
- How do people like to pay for such a product or service? Are they happy with writing checks or giving cash?
- Do you need to set up a business bank account? Ask your bank what their policies are for small business accounts.
- How important is a nice office?
- Do you have enough time to devote to this new business? Can your family be helpfully involved?

With the answers to these questions, she could begin to put a true picture together of how her business should look. She would know who her target clientele was and whether they would come by way of referrals from their friends, doctors, teachers, or counselors or from advertising in the local media. Also, many people still pay with checks and cash, but the majority of people choose to pay with credit and debit cards, and a professional office definitely helps the clientele feel more at ease.

How is that for a different perspective of her new business than the one she had? By finding answers to the above questions before she started, she would have learned a great deal about her business and not spent any money doing it. Also, she would have gained a few referrals just by talking to people who would have become interested in her business.

Her next step would be to find a bookkeeper, an accountant, and a lawyer. Professionals are in the business because they have something to offer. One of the mistakes in business is assuming that you or your friend can do the books to save money. There are a great percentage of enterprises that start off financially well with a great deal of customers but wind up in trouble because of just this. Due to the lack of professional information, the business owners don't realize the importance of things such as paying taxes properly, getting their business names registered, buying insurance, and setting up their business according to the laws. By the time a business has been open for just over a year, lots of these problems become apparent. To start with, many of the problems are manageable; however, if the business actually makes it to the three-year mark, all hell can break loose. According to: Source: Statistics Canada, special tabulations of data from the *Longitudinal Employment Analysis Program* (LEAP), 1994–2003, the percentage of new micro businesses (businesses with less than 5 employees) in the service producing industries that survive to complete one year of business is 76%, by the end of the third year that stat falls to only 48% and after 7 years a dismal 29%.

The next time June is dreaming of starting a business, she should get to this point before she starts. The original money she lost on advertising could have been spent on professional advice, which would have jump-started her business. It would be set up and ready to go, and she wouldn't be scrambling and stressed.

In hindsight, June realized the mistakes she made as she emptied her quaint little office and reduced the size of her business to a home office and the use of a boardroom at an office center. A little planning would have gone a long way. Sorry, June.

Check out the following website where I found a great survey that may help determine if you are ready to open/operate your own small business at: [2]http://www.smallbusinessbc.ca/bizideas-feasibility.php

Pointer: Take responsibility for your business dream. Make your dream a reality by ensuring that your paperwork, accounting, and banking are organized before you put up your business shingle.

[2]**Small Business BC** 601 West Cordova Street Vancouver BC V6B 1G1 Phone: 604-775-5525 In BC: 1- 800- 667-2272 Fax: 604-775-5520 http://www.smallbusinessbc.ca Reviewed: October 2004

IGNORANCE IN BUSINESS
IS A LIABILITY

Often Heard Comment by New Business Owners:
You can pay your employees cash under the table and save money.

Reality:
You may think you are saving money by not processing your payroll legally, but in the long run, you will be traveling down a very dangerous path. What if that employee tells someone, like the government? He or she may not do so maliciously, the revelation may happen very innocently, but as the business owner, you are responsible.

Over the years, I have worked with more than one hundred business owners, who have all asked the same questions. The answers can make or break your business before you get started, which means they are important and should be taken very seriously.

Learn the answers to these questions before *you start your business:*

- Should you incorporate or keep the business as a proprietorship?
- Do you need a business license?
- Should you register your business?
- Should you start your business at home or should you find an office?

- Will you need to sign a lease and if so will you have to give a personal guarantee for a lease?
- How much money will you need to get started?
- What types of receipts will you use?
- How will you make remittances to the government?
- Should you do your own books or do you need an accountant and a bookkeeper?
- How will you advertise?
- Will you need insurance?
- Should you have sales experience before starting your own business?
- What types of beliefs do you have about salespeople?
- Should you have a landline telephone, a cell phone, a fax machine, or an Internet phone?
- Do you need a Web site?

Business is business and should be thought through completely.

The government doesn't care that you don't know what to charge tax on; all they care about is that you do indeed charge tax appropriately. Charging taxes for your products or services is definitely one area that you should take serious precautions with! If you make an error calculating the amount of tax you charge your clients, then you are 100 percent responsible for that error. When the government audits your books (and trust me, they will sooner or later), they will insist that you pay for the shortfall. It comes out of your pocket unless you are able to go back to your clients and have them pay the extra amount owing, and if the bill was from two or three years ago, you may have a problem. Some of the businesses may not even exist anymore and even if they do, they may refuse to pay you and your only choice would be to take them to court.

Government tax offices are filled with information to help businesses. It would be worth taking the time to visit your local tax office to find out requirements for your specific business.

We have all heard stories about companies that have made a ton of money by not paying proper taxes to the government. Just imagine how those same companies feel when their little scheme gets discovered and they have to pay back taxes, plus accumulated interest, and even a penalty.

Please know that sometimes you may get away with doing things in an illegal manner, but the rest of the business world will never take you seriously.

Do you care what the rest of the business community thinks of you? You should! They are your customers too. Or maybe their mother or their child or someone they know is a future customer of yours. Running your business properly is of the utmost importance and can be the one thing that ensures that your dream grows.

So the question that arises is: What makes you think you can open and run a business when so many around you are failing? I have heard dozens of reasons to open a business like: "I want to be more independent." "There is no getting rich working for someone else." "I need more time to spend with my kids." "I hate my job." "Nobody understands me at the office." "I have so many great ideas I just know I will be successful." "I want to do good things for others." And my favorite reason of all: "I want to retire early and this is the only way to do it."

People are in business to make money, and that is the truth. Anyone who tries to tell you otherwise is not being honest. Yes, we all go into business to be our own bosses, work our own hours, and be happy, but if we weren't in search of the almighty dollar, we probably wouldn't have a need to open a business.

Money is good. It feeds us, it provides us with shelter, and it lets us soak in our hot tubs and travel to exotic locations. Why then is there so much negativity around money? Are we greedy for wanting more? Are we evil if we have too much? Does it make us bad people to have lots of money?

My personal belief lies in the notion that we are what we think we are. If we think we are greedy for wanting more, then, yes, we are greedy. If we think we are evil if we have too much, then, yes, we are evil. If we know that money will allow us to become philanthropists to help those in need, then we will see the good in money, as we should.

It is important for all small business owners to understand their attitudes about money. How is it possible to attract money if negative programming or thoughts from our past, our families, or our friends play in our brain?

A couple of my clients say that the most important reason to gain money is to help the poor. They believe that they do not deserve to have more than the poor as that would be inappropriate and would leave them feeling coldhearted. If only they could understand that energy attracts like energy. If your thoughts say money makes you coldhearted, then how are you ever going to attract more money, unless, of course, you wish to be coldhearted?

If a scenario like this is playing in your brain, there are ways to change your thinking. One of the best ways is to write a journal. Now don't roll your eyes and think, *Oh, she sounds like a counselor.* Just hear what I'm trying to say. Write down all of your feelings about money. There is no wrong answer, so it does not matter what you write. Maybe you lived in poverty as a child and are afraid of starving; maybe your friends had lots of money to spend and you had none. The most important thing is to write anything that comes to mind and write until you are tired of writing. Then read over all of the words you have written. You may shock yourself when you start to learn your true feelings about money.

And, the really cool thing is that none of us are exactly the same. No one in this world thinks like you because you were the only one brought up in your environment. Even if you had a twin who was brought up in the exact same family and surroundings, your perceptions would differ. Your thoughts belong to you, and absolutely no one can influence your thoughts unless you allow him or her to.

And this doesn't just apply to your attitude about money and making your business financially successful for both you and your employees. You'll also find creating and conveying a positive attitude makes a huge difference when it comes to finding and recruiting potential customers. Once your business is up and running and you've established a customer base.

Try to look deep into yourself and understand what it is that you truly want from your business. Once you've identified your needs and beliefs, you will have the greatest groundwork imaginable from which to grow a business. You may not realize how important your thoughts are to others. When they hear you excited about your business and your life, they'll want the same results. This is how you help people; you lead by example.

On the other hand, if people hear you complaining about or arguing with your customers, they may be wary about doing business with you. If you tell a potential customer a negative story about another customer in hopes of getting a sympathy vote, do not be surprised if you lose both customers. It doesn't matter if you were ripped off or if you were the one who was right. You just demoted yourself from professional businessperson to whiner and complainer. The potential customer may just walk out the door in search of a more positive experience.

Also, know that you will never force someone to think like you do, especially your customer. The best thing is to listen to what the customer is telling you. Try very hard not to let your own personal bias come into play—just hear your customer's words and think of him or her. Keep your thoughts positive and kind in order to provide the most effective feedback that you can to find an idea or solution that suits your customer as an individual. By practicing this positive thinking, you will send out positive emotions that will attract a client base that is warm and friendly. Plus, your existing clients will be happy to work with you because you make them feel good.

Pointer: Due diligence—learn what it means and do it. Maybe the government may never find out that you paid your employees "under the table," but what happens at the end of the year when your accountant asks you where the cash went? It may end up becoming part of your personal income, and you may need to pay personal tax on it.

SALES ARE EASY TO FIND

Often Heard Comment by New Business Owners:
*The business I want to open will have tons of sales; the idea is
brilliant, so I can't lose.*

Reality:
*It is a very exhilarating prospect to own a business, and the
excitement often leads people to overlook the obvious. Where
exactly will the sales come from? If you are a terrible salesperson,
it may be time to learn what it takes to bring in the sales.*

Your business is up running, and everything is going as planned. It feels
good, doesn't it? There is one problem—the sales. Where are the sales?
Where are all the customers? How do they know your business exists?

Take a step back and look at your creation. What could you do
that would make a difference? What could you do to create excitement
or to create a need for your potential clients?

The real estate world offers a great example of creating need for
potential customers. It doesn't take an engineer to see how new condo
developments constantly create excitement and the consumers almost
always respond. They create phases of the development and release
one phase of condos for sale at a time. Not only does this help the
developer to gain cash flow for building, but it also creates urgency for
the potential buyers. The big signs at construction sites often note that
the condos are "75 % sold out," and our first reaction is often, *What
am I missing out on?* It may be only phase one that is 75 percent sold
out, but it still gets our attention and increases our curiosity.

All businesses benefit from knowing why their product is better than the competitors', which is the starting point for creating customer need. It works for small businesses of all types, including massage therapy, bookkeeping, financial planning, lawn cutting, counseling, snow plowing, and sales of all kinds. When customers need your products or services, your business must offer value to them, which means that, as a small business owner you need to know your customers. Once you know their needs, you can create a marketing or promotional plan to help increase the desire for the product.

The health industry provides many opportunities for lucrative small businesses. One such business is massage therapy. How can a Licensed Massage Therapist (LMT) increase her customer base? First, like all other small business owners, the LMT places an advertisement in the local paper and telephone book, which is the easy part. These ads interest a few clients, and the business begins to grow. As the LMT desperately waits for the necessary income required to pay the office rent, the advertising, and the telephone bill, she may begin to question her decision to go to school for three years and open a business. She may even begin experiencing serious self-doubt and asks herself: *Who do I think I am? I have never run a business before. Maybe I should quit now before things get too bad. What will I tell my friends? I don't want to be a failure. Why did I quit my job?*

This is the perfect time to take some serious action. A massage therapist needs to let people know who and where she is. A small letter to all of the local doctors, chiropractors, and physiotherapists in town is an excellent way to introduce a new business in the health industry. But for a massage therapist, the person doing the massage is just as important as the name and location of the business. Massage therapy is a specialty service provided by an individual person, and this person can make a big impact on the rate at which she gains clientele by hand delivering the letters. This is where fear and negative thoughts often set in. The new therapist may find herself thinking: *What if the doctor doesn't want to talk to me? What if he or she doesn't have time to see me? What if one of the doctors laughs at me?* The sad reality is that some might actually laugh at her, but odds are in her favor that they won't. Most doctors want to know who provides different types of services in their communities in order to refer their own patients to the best care possible.

Here's a proven way to get over this hurdle. If the doctor is unavailable, introduce yourself to the receptionist or front desk attendant and talk to that person as you would to the doctor. Never ever underestimate the importance of the person at the front desk because that person has more power than you could ever imagine. The person at the front desk is often referred to in sales as "the gatekeeper," and your entire goal as a salesperson, for you and your business, is getting past the gatekeeper. The gatekeeper will tell the doctor his or her impression of you, whether you were kind and compassionate or bossy and crabby. Making friends with the gatekeeper will go a very long way toward having the doctor refer patients to you.

A great friend and successful small business owner named Pat has helped me to understand just what made her business work. Pat is a Registered Massage Therapist with a clientele that keeps her working as many hours as she has to offer.

"The most important thing I did was join a networking group, which helped me to be more confident and learn how to network," said Pat. The networking group helped Pat to become comfortable speaking about herself and her business without feeling that she was bragging. She had no problem introducing herself at doctor's offices and found that most offices were happy that she had come in.

Pat spent three full years in school learning her trade. She learned how to give therapeutic massages and also how to set up and maintain a small business. Before she even started her business, she had a business plan ready to go.

She began her practice in a chiropractic clinic so she could capitalize on the referrals from other professionals. The owners of the chiropractic clinic insisted that she use their company name and logo on all of her correspondence; plus, they supplied her with a billing system for insurance-related items and basically put everything in place for scheduling and regular client payments. From Pat's perspective, this was an excellent way to get started, but the major drawback was cost. The costs were extremely high and Pat always felt she was paying far too much money for the services she was receiving. That's when Pat joined the networking group and suddenly everything began to change. The networking group was very professionally organized with its referral system, and it did not take long before Pat's client base started to increase.

One of the members of the networking group introduced Pat to a packaged office (a place where she could choose and pay for only the services she needed like a small office with reception and telephone answering rather than opening her own clinic) that was just in the start-up stages. Pat did some research and found that the packaged office might be just what she was searching for to lower her costs and make her business more profitable. The thought of moving her practice from the safe, professional environment she had known was quite terrifying and forced her to make her decision slowly. Could she really make a go of this on her own? There was so much work and planning to do, but once she made her decision, she knew she could do it and decided it would be worth it in the long run.

Pat gave a one-month notice to the chiropractic clinic, and while continuing to care for her existing clients, spent her spare time preparing for the move. She sent an easy-to-read, one-page flyer to all of her clients and friends; plus she offered a coupon to all customers for the following two months. She promoted herself by letting people know she was opening her own clinic and that she was very excited. All of Pat's existing clients wanted to see the new location, so Pat was inevitably busy in her new clinic and many of the clients were so impressed they shared their coupons with their friends.

The move to the new location was just what Pat wanted and more. She was able to provide her clients with excellent care in a very professional environment at a much lower cost than at the chiropractic clinic. This was phase two of her business, and it flourished. Not only did Pat create a successful business, she also had a busy and exciting personal life. With her office in the new location for about one year, she and her husband bought a house with a yard so their baby daughter could have a place to run around. It only took a short time to settle into their new love nest; soon, they started planning to have another baby.

Having the business itself would have been enough to keep me up at night, so I asked Pat how she intended to keep her business up and running while being pregnant, taking maternity leave, and then raising her two children. She wasn't really sure what she would do, so she started to research how she could do it all, pay the bills, and still make money to live on. She interviewed massage therapists until she found two who would be appropriate to fill in for her during her pregnancy. Once she found her replacements, she set up all the paperwork to ensure her rent and payroll would be met; organized the schedule, giving herself about five months of maternity leave; and comfortably looked forward to the birth of her baby.

She had a beautiful baby boy. It wasn't easy for Pat to do all of this, but she had such a terrific attitude—she never doubted it would all work out.

After the birth of her son, Pat learned one of the most unexpected lessons of her business career. She learned a simple way to create a need for her services when she wasn't even trying. Early in her career, Pat worked five days per week and occasionally six, but with two small children at home, she chose to reduce her workdays to three so she could be with her children as much as possible. What a surprise she had when, practically overnight, her business increased, and so did her income. Clients were so worried that she wouldn't have time to see them that they booked appointments like crazy. Plus another terrific thing happened: Her clients started to really value Pat as an expert in her field. She no longer tolerated clients missing appointments and always enforced a payment plan for missed appointments.

Once Pat started to learn her own value in both her business and her personal life, her boundaries became better, and she naturally poised herself in a continual learning and bettering cycle. Being confident about the services she provided showed current and potential customers that she was proud of her work, that she did a good job, and that her skills were very sought after.

Confidence in business appears to be the secret to success for many people. If a client sees your schedule and realizes that you are not very busy, this can easily lead him or her to believe that you are not very good. If you only have one client in the whole world and want to have more, do not let that one client know it. Schedule your time in advance and put any appointment or meeting you may have in your date book, even if it is an appointment to take your mouse to the veterinarian. Set aside exclusive times for your business and only stay available at those times.

Another great idea for appointment bookings is to always ask the client when he or she might be available and then offer two specific time options. For example: "Would you like to see me on Monday or Tuesday? Do you prefer mornings or afternoons? Would you like to come in at 9:00 or 11:30?"

Set the boundaries for your business because, if you don't, your clients will try to do it for you, and that will stress you out, which in turn tends to repel customers. By setting standards and rules and boundaries, you will stay in control of your business and continue to feel the excitement of a new business owner.

Many years ago, I read a letter to the editor written by a person we will call Sandy who had purchased a retail business with a storefront in a small town. When Sandy wrote the letter, he had been in business for approximately one year. The letter sounded very angry as he lashed out at the community for requesting donations from him but not shopping in the store. It was obvious that Sandy was short on money, short on patience, and afraid that his business was not going to make it. It also became evident that he had nowhere to turn, so he cashed in his "victim" card and blamed the community (his customers) for his problems.

My immediate reaction was, unfortunately, one of anger because I had felt the same way when I first started my business. I was angry because I had chosen a different route than Sandy. I had asked for advice and found a way to ensure that my business became successful! And I had not blamed the community for my initial fears that my business might not succeed.

I wrote a letter to the editor in response, in the same angry tone that Sandy had written his. Here is an excerpt from my letter:

> *From all of the statistics I have read, most companies have trouble making it past the first year of business, especially retail, and if they can make it past the third year they are doing very well.*
>
> *Congratulations on celebrating your 1st year anniversary; I am surprised that you stayed in business this long.*
>
> *Personally, I think that lashing out at the specific community you are trying to attract is one quick way to alienate customers, especially during such an important gift-giving season as Christmas.*
>
> *Instead of blaming others for your problems, try looking at the way you attract business:*

- *Is your store name appropriate to attract both the female and male genders?*
- *Do you have an appropriate advertising campaign?*
- *If you are targeting a specific market, does your community have enough interest to sustain your business?*
- *Is there any way you can market your business elsewhere while keeping your storefront?*
- *Do you offer any referral incentives to your current customers?*

In retrospect, it would have been better to write the letter from a position of kindness rather than anger, as I would have felt better and perhaps been more helpful. The great news is that, as of this writing, Sandy is still in business and, according to a mutual acquaintance, it was my letter that woke him up and helped him find a way to make his business successful. Does that mean I know better than anyone else? Not a chance. What I do know is how to be proactive when it comes to business.

My friend, Freddy, has a small restaurant that caters to the breakfast and lunch crowd. Freddy bought the restaurant at a time when the economy was very strong; he had many customers, and employees were plentiful.

It is a labor of love for Freddy to run his restaurant. He loves to cook, especially for those people who appreciate his flair for fine cuisine. He didn't exactly make his dreams come true when he bought the restaurant; yet, he reasoned with himself that it was his first step toward becoming a chef in his own fine restaurant.

Freddy came to me for advice early one Monday morning; he had been forced to close his restaurant for the day due to lack of staff. The economy was faltering a bit, and weirdly enough, employees were hard to find. He would have had over two hundred customers that day, and it hurt his business to be closed during his busiest day of the week.

My thoughts for Freddy are the same for all small companies. Do your best to be prepared for a crisis like this and be adaptable to odd situations. I know planning for the unexpected is easier said than done, so here are the ideas I offered Freddy:

For one day, change the set up of the restaurant. Instead of the normal, full service offered, have the customers place his or her order at the kitchen, take a number, and then come pick up the meal when it is ready. This obviously has shades of a cafeteria but only for a short period of time, and with proper communication, the new arrangement could just save the day. The daily special sign could be modified for the day to let customers know what is going on:

5% OFF
<u>TODAY'S MEAL</u>

We are short-staffed and
do not want to close.

So, for today only, we ask that you walk up to
the kitchen area and place your order.

And for fun, tell the cook a joke and win a free
meal!

(The cook is the judge and will give
one free meal each hour.)

For Freddy, the next day was an absolute blast. He still hadn't found a server, so he put his new plan in place, changed his specials sign, and spent a ton of time talking to the customers. Everyone told him he was crazy, and his customers were thrilled with the change to their day. Some people even phoned their friends and told them what was going on. Freddy had more customers than normal because the locals wanted to see what was happening.

The 5 percent taken off of everyone's bill and the free meals Freddy gave away were compensated by the fact that Freddy didn't have his two employees to pay that day. The profit was the same, the customers had fun, and even though Freddy had to work harder than normal, he was happy to keep the restaurant open. Freddy kept his customers at his restaurant instead of losing them to the competition and got to show the community that he could handle adversity and have fun doing it. Obviously this scenario wouldn't work for all restaurants. This is just one businessperson's example of adapting in a crisis.

Preparation for the future should also include planning for possible problems. Freddy chose to write a "What to do in a Crisis" Manual.

The manual was nothing spectacular; it was just a binder with paper in it. He listed a bunch of potential issues for his restaurant and then added the solutions. On quiet days, Freddy worked on his manual and included his staff in the process. He knew that his employees were his best assets, and they often came up with brilliant ideas that he would never have thought of.

Reflecting back on his dreams of a fine restaurant, Freddy realized that his existing experience was quite pleasurable and profitable. The restaurant of his dreams was the one he was currently running. Perhaps the table linens were made of polyester, and most customers didn't wear suits and ties, but that hadn't stopped Freddy from considering hiring an entertainer once in a while to change things up a bit.

Here is one of Freddy's brilliant ideas that also deals with being short-staffed in the kitchen: If a cook doesn't show up for work, rather than making the diners wait extra long for their food and perhaps making regulars angry, Freddy plans to limit the menu. For this occasion, he will also offer a 5 percent discount and perhaps add a twist for a few free meals. This is how his menu will read:

5% OFF BECAUSE
<u>WE ONLY HAVE ONE COOK TODAY</u>

Today's Breakfast Menu:
Scrambled Eggs & Toast
With Bacon and Pan-fried Spuds
Coffee/Tea or Juice

OR

Toasted Bacon & Tomato Sandwich
With Pan-fried Spuds
Coffee/Tea or Juice

Enter our drawing for:
One free meal each hour until the cook comes
back

This solution is so very simple that it doesn't seem like it would work. So, to confirm his plan, Freddy has discussed it with many of his regular customers, and the response has been overwhelmingly positive.

Pointer: Don't sit and wait for customers to find you; do something to help *them find you. Offer referrals, offer discounts, send out letters, make phone calls—bring the customers to you.*

TAXES, EMPLOYEES, HONESTY, AND GOVERNMENT

Often Heard Comment by New Business Owners:
You own a business; you can write that purchase off.

Reality:
Yes, you can write off certain items that are used specifically for your business, but you still have to pay for them first. The money comes out of your pocket—out of your profit. "Writing something off" does not mean that it is free; you still have to pay for it.

A very important part of business is honesty. Keep your business, your books, and your employees honest. Find a way to make it work. If you are candid, truthful, and think honestly, then you will attract likeminded customers

My first foray into hiring an employee almost created a disaster for my company. My business had reached a stage where I was no longer able to do all of the work myself. I needed help. I needed to take a break once in a while.

I hired someone I knew. She was intelligent and friendly, but within a couple of months, I realized that she was a social butterfly and had no intention of doing any real work. I would walk out the office door on an errand, and she would walk away from the front desk and visit with everyone in the office. She always said she had so much to do during the day that she could not get any extra work done. She was often late for work and left early. She really had no desire to be an employee for an up-and-coming small business.

I spent countless hours training her and even tried to find projects to suit her. I asked if she was creative, and she told me she didn't understand what I meant. I asked what she did in her spare time, and she answered that she visited with her friends. The effort I made to help this woman help me was far beyond what I should have made. I continued to ask about her interests: Did she bake? Did she like cooking? Was she a gardener? Did she enjoy painting, golfing, or reading? You name it, I asked it; and the answer was always the same: "No, I really only like to hang out with my friends and perhaps shop." This woman was forty-eight years old. How had she survived in the workforce for this long?

Once I became aware that she had no interest in herself, I realized that she would not make it as an employee in my business. Yet I still needed help. I set out to hire someone else. I felt like an impostor. My business had been open for about six months, and I still didn't feel like it was mine. I made decisions and worked hard and still looked around for the boss to take over.

When a client came to me with someone she thought would be perfect for the job, I jumped at the chance. So, suddenly I had to get rid of the employee who didn't care and replace her with one who cared a great deal but who had virtually no skills, was totally technology-phobic, and couldn't work on her own.

By now, my pattern has probably become quite obvious. Take the easy road and hope like heck it will all work out. With both employees being part-time, I slowly phased out the original one, which worked out well because she had found a job she liked better. Whew!

Tax time was coming up and the original employee phoned me virtually every day for her tax paperwork. And there I sat, living in complete fear. I had been doing all of the books myself. All payroll deductions were done correctly, but I had never properly signed up to remit the deductions to the government for my employee. What in the world was I going to do? I thought of every possible lying and cheating scenario and could not come up with a solution. I had no extra money as the business start-up had taken most of it, so how would I afford professional help to solve my problem?

Just as I thought things would get no worse, I received a letter from the government advising me that I was about to be audited. If I'd thought I was afraid before, well now I was completely terrified. What was I going to do? How could I get around this? I didn't sleep for one entire week. I was angry, frustrated, and depressed.

One day, I went for a walk to clear my head, and the solution suddenly dawned on me. I had to face reality and be honest. It was time to stop running away and learn the correct way to do business. I also knew there would be a repercussion to everything I had been doing, and I decided to accept whatever was coming. This was the moment when I became a true business owner! This was the moment that changed my future, as I stopped acting like a victim and took full responsibility for my decisions.

Who knew that honesty could be so freeing? I had made the right decision. I hired a bookkeeper and was surprised to learn that her services didn't really cost very much. She went through all of my records and processed the entire payroll, employment insurance, and the pension payments properly. The proper paperwork went out on time, which was just plain lucky, and the bookkeeper told me to relax about the upcoming audit. She advised that I would probably pay a penalty to the government for the payroll issues, and that should be the worst of it.

Finally the day of the audit came. My heart was pounding so hard that I thought it would explode. The audit didn't last very long, much to my surprise, and when it was all over, I was assessed a penalty of twenty dollars.

That was it—twenty dollars; what an incredible relief. I'd lost so much sleep trying to find ways to cheat that it was quite amazing to learn that the penalty was so low. Had I tried to hide what I was doing, it would have all backfired, and I probably would have lost the whole company.

From that moment on, I have made every effort to be honest and legitimate in business and always follow the rules. I trust my inner voice now and stick to my morals. My accounting books are accurate, which perhaps doesn't always make for glowing financial statements, but I live in peace knowing that I did the right things, that I came clean with the audit, and that I have no fear of retroactive repercussions. In the future, when the business is sold, the financial statements will be accurate, and I will be able to provide a complete and true picture of the organization. This decision may not suit everyone in the business world, but peace of mind and living a calm life mean much more to me than a couple of extra bucks.

So, business was getting better, but my second employee really needed to go. As a person, she was wonderful, but as an employee, she was a stinker. I finally, very sadly, let her go on a Friday afternoon— that's how I'd always heard firing needed to be done.

For the next six months, the business became my sole responsibility. I needed to set procedures and rules so that, when I did hire another employee, he or she wouldn't be expected to read my mind; my new employee would have paperwork to follow, and the job would be much easier.

One of my business friends, Myrna Park, taught me how to hire an employee. She began by letting me know that it was my responsibility to decide:

- The type of person I would like to hire
- The skills that would be required to do the job
- The amount of training I would provide
- Exactly how many hours he or she would work
- The degree of responsibility on the job

You will be amazed by what you'll learn as a businessperson by answering these questions in advance. I learned that, if I couldn't identify what my needs were, then I would never be able to achieve my goal.

By this time, I had been in business almost two years. I knew how to create and operate my business, and I knew exactly how much income I would bring in at each stage of the business. But I had absolutely no goal. My business plan ended after eighteen months, and I had no planned direction. Well, honestly, I did have one goal—I wanted to make lots of money. I had no idea how much money was lots, but I kind of thought that one million dollars sounded good.

Once I identified my employee needs, I put an advertisement in the paper and waited for résumés. I went back to Myrna, who told me that I had to follow up with references; plus, I needed to write a list of questions that I wanted each candidate to answer. This was turning out to be far more work than had I imagined, but when I remembered the first two employees I'd hired, I decided that the work would be worth it.

I interviewed three people, chose the one best suited for the job, had her do a computer test (that I created myself), and phoned her references. One of her references was terrible. I was shocked and didn't know what to do. After all that work, the thought of starting over again left me frustrated and almost ready to give up. Fortunately, Myrna came to the rescue. She told me to dig deeper in the résumé and find a different way to get references. So I phoned places where my future employee had worked and learned that the person who had given the bad reference was simply doing it out of spite.

This time, my choice of employee was good. I had chosen a great person with great references, and I hired her immediately. As of this writing, she is still my employee, and I highly value her skills and her opinion.

Pointer: Take care to check skills, backgrounds, and ambitions of potential employees, even if you feel that you are too busy to do so. The easy way is seldom the best choice for your business.

OTHER PEOPLE'S MONEY

Often Heard Comment by New Business Owners:
Start up a company using other people's money; there's no need to use your own.

Reality:
Using other people's money sounds like a terrific idea, if you can get away with it. If you have been in business for years or you have a very good track record with solid contacts who trust you, it may be possible to find an investor, but you will still need to use some of your own capital. You can borrow against your credit cards or even take a loan from the bank, but it's still considered your money—you have to pay it back.

There are a great many books written about how to do business; many of them make sense to me, and many leave me feeling that I have no idea what I am doing running a corporation. When I opened my first business, I was a long way from understanding how a business should run. Also, I continued to question myself, wondering what the heck I thought I was doing. Who was I to open a business when so many others around me had failed? Negative books and media had me thinking that I would never make it in business; it drove me crazy to think that I could spend so much time and money on a project just to have it fall by the wayside because I didn't know what I was doing.

This fear did not stop me from educating myself with great books that actually applied to my business, my thought patterns, and my goals. It was important to realize that none of us were the same in this world of commerce. We all thought differently. That is what makes the world so very interesting. Why strive to be average? Try to understand your true nature and find an industry that makes you excited about day-to-day enterprise.

The books that always scared me were the ones advising how to do business by using other people's money. Not having to spend your own money sounded like a very wonderful concept, and it's a great idea if you can manage it; but when you look at the statistics of businesses making it past their first year from Chapter Two of this book; you realize that something is wrong with the picture.

Bernice was a client who thought my business ideas were out of style and way behind the times. Why? Because I do not spend money I don't have, and I prefer not to use credit. Bernice insisted that my business would never grow if I tried to grow it slowly.

Bernice was a well-educated businesswoman with amazing ideas. Her sales skills were excellent, and her business idea was sound and had great potential; plus it had some planning behind it. She had a business adviser who knew exactly what she needed to do, and she listened to everything he said. She hired him after making a cold call to his office and did not check his references. Little did she know at the time that her business adviser was not well liked in the community and had made many of his past clients angry and determined to never use his services again.

A lack of money did not stop Bernice from spending on credit, and she was not worried in the least. With the help of her adviser, she decided that branding her business, getting a fabulous Web site, choosing the right office space, hiring the right employees, preparing for future clients, and advertising would be the most important items. She hired six employees and was ready to hire more.

She had been in business about three months when her business partner decided he wanted to sell the building that housed the business, and he also wanted to quit his share of the partnership. It was a blow to Bernice, but she was a resourceful woman who wasn't about to stop, especially when she had such a great business plan laid out.

Being the incredible salesperson that she was, Bernice found new office space almost immediately, bought furniture on credit, moved her employees and equipment, and even found a new business partner. The new partner was from out of the country and did not speak English as well as Bernice would have liked, but he did have a fair amount of business knowledge and had the money required to get the business going.

She had to move fast because it was time for the holiday she had scheduled—a full month away with her boyfriend—and she wanted the business in good hands before she left. She would be in constant communication with her employees and partner through e-mail, video conferencing, Internet, and telephone, so her business would not suffer. She would use all the high-tech communication tools that were available to her and run her business while she was away.

Before she left on holiday, she gained four customers, all of whom believed in her dream as much as she did. She had also created a procedure manual to ensure the existing customers' needs were met but didn't have much of a plan for creating new customers while she was away. Her business revolved around her and her sales skills. All of her employees used English as a second language and were not able to effectively communicate well enough to gain new customers in their adopted country.

Why did she use employees who were still learning English? She knew that the people she hired were intelligent and well educated in their home countries; plus she could pay these same people low wages, as they had found it difficult to gain employment.

The four customers who Bernice had acquired before her holiday brought in one-fiftieth of the money required to get the business started, let alone sustain and pay the employee's wages. When Bernice excitedly arrived back to work from her holiday, she learned that no new customers were on board. But she was still so excited about her future that a lack of customers didn't seem to hold her back. While she was on holiday she had decided to move to another city a thousand miles away and open another division of her company. She wanted to be close to her boyfriend and still run the business she had worked so hard to start.

It was not a surprise to learn that her new business partner was more than a bit skeptical as she explained her latest idea. He had assumed that she would come back to the company and bring in all the sales they so desperately needed. Instead, he was about to learn that Bernice knew how to plan like crazy but had no idea about the importance of follow-through; nor did she have a good, solid work ethic.

However, Bernice was one heck of a salesperson, so she had no problem convincing her business partner that it would all work out. She was planning to buy a house in the new city and start the second office in her home. That would save on expenses and the business would grow faster than she had originally planned. A local car dealership gave her a loan on a new vehicle because her business adviser vouched for her, and surely the business would have no problem making a car payment.

Gaining sales in the original business location would be a problem, so she and her business partner decided to hire a manager. The manager would be paid wages plus profit sharing, so the advertised position appeared very enticing. They hired a highly skilled person, did a couple of days of training, and told the manager that the company was hers to manage.

Feeling that all was in place, Bernice loaded up her truck and moved to the new city. The drive would take approximately four days, and she would not take any time to rest, as she was ready to get to work. Her boyfriend had stopped calling about three weeks earlier, but that did not deter her. She was bound and determined to make this work, boyfriend or not.

About halfway to her destination, everything began to go wrong. The newly hired business manager had a serious look at the books when no one was around, and she figured out that the company had no money, and it was up to her to make it work. The manager realized that there would be no guaranteed pay check with this company, so she quit, leaving Bernice and her business partner with no manager.

What was Bernice going to do? She phoned her business adviser and did exactly what he said—she hired him to bring in the sales. He would do the sales in advance and work out a payment schedule. His smarmy, old-fashioned, snake oil salesman technique was rather offensive, and within about one week, Bernice and her partner had lost one of their four existing clients.

Around this same time, Bernice's business partner started to feel like he was being used. He wished his English skills were better so he could increase the sales because he didn't like working with Bernice's adviser. He also started to realize that, without his money, there would be no company. He laid off most of the employees.

A month later, there were still no sales being brought into the company. Bernice wasn't having much success setting up her company in the new city where she didn't know anyone and had absolutely no business contacts, so she decided to take a job at ten dollars an hour while she got organized.

Bernice's business partner decided to leave the business and phoned Bernice with his final date. Bernice e-mailed her landlord and instructed him to sell all of her furniture and equipment then send her a check. Once again, she was confident that she could use the money to get started in her new city.

The landlord pretty much laughed at Bernice, as he informed her that she had signed a legal, one-year lease on her office, and he intended on seizing all of her assets to pay the debt. Bernice phoned her lawyer, only to realize that the landlord was right. She didn't have a legal leg to stand on, and it was time for her to face the facts. This business was about to become a statistic and close for good.

Bernice believed everything she had read about how to create and run a business and just couldn't understand why her business had to fold. She blamed all of the problems on the people she had hired and partnered with, rather than taking a good look at her role in the situation. The business had been doomed to fail from its inception. Her idea was solid and well thought out, and the original planning she had done was excellent, but she never followed through with the development of customers. She didn't want to do the work. She wanted to be rich and famous and let other people do the work for her.

Wanting everyone who's involved in a company to work hard toward the end goal is not such a bad desire, but the person at the top with the great idea needs to find a way to share it with everyone else. The rest of the people involved in the company need to understand the vision and how it will be obtained with direction from the one person who understands it. Once everyone understands the direction, each person can begin to follow by example.

Unfortunately for Bernice, the business she was running ended within eight months of its beginning because she had no desire to do the start-up work and show the employees how great her idea was.

The questions I asked in retrospect were: Why spend money that you don't have? You will just have to pay it back some day with interest. Are you able to work with what you already have? Is there an affordable way to gain some knowledge of your own to ensure you are on the right path?

Let's take a look at how Bernice could have started her business; we'll see an entirely different picture. She could have begun her business from a home office and hired one employee and still gained and retained the four customers she had. There are many places that provide virtual office services with a day office or boardroom for a low fee as well as secretarial services, faxing, and copying. Instead of losing thousands of dollars all at once, she could have grown her business slowly and made money. A small business with a home office certainly doesn't sound very glamorous and may not be all that exciting to tell friends, but it is so much more fun to be successful after a couple of years rather than bankrupt in a few months.

My friend, Mike, told me how he started his thriving landscaping business. Mike's story is one of humble beginnings, which will hopefully motivate others to similar greatness. All he had when he started was a lawn mower and a truck and a great desire to run an enterprise of his own.

Mike is charming and charismatic and loves talking to people. For him, asking for sales was a simple and comfortable experience and not much different from day-to-day living. He talked to every home owner in his neighborhood and offered to cut their lawns on an ongoing basis. Out of his neighborhood, he found two people willing to pay him to cut their lawns. Mike was in business!

Yes, it can be that simple to be a businessperson. Perhaps cutting lawns for the neighbors doesn't sound very enchanting, but Mike was earning an income the same day he went into business, and he didn't owe anyone money.

As he went about his work, he noticed his new customer's garden was overgrown with weeds, so he offered to clean it up for extra money. And lo and behold, the customer said yes. Mike did a meticulous job on both lawns and the garden and was proud of a job well done. Two days later, a person down the street asked Mike if he had time to work on his elderly mother's yard a couple of miles away, and of course Mike, said yes. Then, after he completed that job, he knocked on the doors of everyone in that neighborhood and gained one more customer. Not bad results for being in business for only a week.

Mike knew he had something good going on, so he kept on knocking on doors. Within one month, Mike had so much business that he had to hire a part-time employee, and he still didn't owe anyone money. I can never express enough how wonderful it is to be in a moneymaking business without needing credit. An income with no debts is like a dream come true for many people, especially when starting up a business. You never have to worry about paying bills because you don't have any. All of your income is yours except the portion that needs to go to the government for taxes. Always remember to pay your taxes properly so you do not have problems in the future.

Occasionally Mike would require a tool he didn't have for a special job. He found a company that would allow him to rent the equipment he needed, and he always paid the bill when he returned the tools. Having access to more tools allowed Mike to diversify and begin providing irrigation services and full landscaping services.

In the winter, Mike would offer snow shoveling to all of his clients, so he had an income in the off-season and also was able to keep in contact with his customers. The business was growing; Mike was learning how to deal with government and taxes, manage employees, and bid on larger jobs. He saved money and purchased his own equipment so he could stop paying for rentals

Mike's wife, Lisa, was also a great advocate of the business. She spoke about her husband's business, abilities, and goals to all of her friends at the coffee shop where she worked. Unbeknownst to Lisa, she told the story to the wife of a business executive in charge of a large development company. About six months later, Mike received a call from the development company asking if he would be interested in bidding on the landscape work for the first phase of their master-planned residential community.

I am sure you have already surmised that Mike won the contract and started the work. As always, his work was meticulous and professional and, of course, the development company was thrilled with the results.

As of this writing, it had been about six years since Mike started cutting lawns. During this time, he had achieved success beyond most people's dreams. But Mike expected the best, provided the best he could, and knew that, with a little time and a lot of effort, his dreams would be fulfilled.

Pointer: Start your business within your means; keep your money in the bank and save it for the future. Even if you declare bankruptcy (some refer

43

to this incorrectly as the easy way out), you'll still have a ton of liability and will definitely lose credibility, not to mention the fact that your actions will hurt other people.

TO PARTNER OR NOT

Often Heard Comment by New Business Owners:
My friend and I get along so well. I am sure we will make terrific partners.

Reality:
A partner in business is like having a life partner. Communication or lack thereof can make or break the relationship. Put everything in writing, including who does what and learn each other's strengths and weaknesses. Sales is a big hurdle for some, and hoping that your partner is good in sales when his or her job for the last ten years has been a shepherd is just plain ridiculous.

I know a gentleman named Reg who is the sole owner and operator of a business that sells specialty widgets. It is well over seven years since Reg and two partners created their extra special product, which is a success story in itself; however, how they've kept the business operating successfully all this time is the part of their story that I'll focus on.

Reg and his partner, or should I say partners, went into this business with their eyes wide open. Reg had had partnerships before, so he knew that having a business partner was like being in a marriage, but the scary part was that Reg's two partners were actually married. The business started off with a bang; the town was thrilled with the trio's product, and local sales were easy. They really felt they were onto something exciting. They put together a business plan, went to the bank, borrowed money to manufacture the product, and, wow, they were in business.

Reg's office was in his home, where he and his wife raised two wonderful kids, and it was always a challenge for Reg to find the time to work on his new business. He found himself staying up late into the night to do all the necessary planning and paperwork that was required to get this business successfully off the ground. As Reg worked diligently on the important things for the business, his partners spent their time dreaming of being rich. The husband and wife partners were contrasting people who didn't agree on much. One of them walked around all the time saying that everything was awesome; his enthusiasm was infectious, and he was fun to be around. His wife, on the other hand, was a woman who always wanted to be in control of the business. This corporation was on shaky ground before it began because the partners were not very good at communicating with one another. The three each owned one-third of the incorporated business. What this meant is that the husband and wife discussed their decisions in the privacy of their own home and then proceeded to force their ideas on Reg.

As a birthday present for Reg, they decided that he needed an office away from his home. They reasoned that Reg should then have lots of time to grow the business to the size that they dreamed about. They leased an office space, moved in furniture, hooked up the telephones, and brought Reg in to see his surprise. Reg was surprised all right—the couple had spent lots of the company's money to open an office, which they then presented as a gift. Reg had no say in this choice, as his partners had assumed that it was a perfect decision. How in the world could Reg complain about the great costs when they had put a big bow on the door and sang "Happy Birthday"? He decided to keep his mouth shut and try to be thankful.

Sadly enough for Reg, he should have spoken up because this was just the beginning of a spending spree that his two partners embarked upon. The partners decided that, with Reg comfortably situated in his lovely new office, the sales would start pouring in, so they could spend as much money as they wanted. After a couple of months, they couldn't understand why the sales were slow and they were not getting rich. Maybe they needed a salesman. So, once again they went and got Reg a surprise—a retired, outright annoying salesman who thought it was OK to discount the product just to make the sale. It didn't matter to him that he was selling the product for less than the cost to make it; he was doing his job bringing in the sales.

About one month later, the partnership blew up. The only way the business would go forward would be for someone to buy the company outright and get rid of the other partners, which is exactly what Reg did. It was a tough decision for him because, although he knew the product was good and he knew there was success in his future, at the same time he was worried about the financial burden he would be taking on.

So Reg did some of his own planning. When he got his financing for the business, he also chose to purchase more equipment to help supplement any future ups and downs. The extra equipment helped him create income during the off-season, when sales were slow. The plan worked perfectly, as he had created an income that would keep the business profitable during all times of the year. Reg put his own twist on the company by being a kind and dependable businessman who people enjoyed doing business with. All changes to the business were well thought out, and all costs were kept to a minimum.

After one successful year in business without partners, Reg began exporting his product out of the country, which minimized his slow season by allowing him to sell to warmer locations during the winter months. He had and still has many ideas and plans for how to keep his business moving forward. As of this writing, he is progressive and optimistic about his future. Reg has also stated that he will never venture into a business partnership again. He has learned to trust in his own abilities and instincts.

In retrospect, Reg and his partners might have worked successfully had they done more preliminary planning. Their initial discussions and business planning needed to include their personal strengths. As a bystander, I saw clearly the roles that each could have played. Reg was a solid, hard worker who knew how to get things done. He was very resourceful, had lots of great contacts, and he knew the ins and outs of the products better than anyone. As to his two partners, the husband was an amazing salesman, and the wife was excellent at administration and organization. They really did have the makings of a successful partnership because of their diverse skills. However, communication breakdown became their demise.

Being able to stand back and see themselves in action would have been a revealing exercise. Had they reached out for help, perhaps to a business coach or someone more knowledgeable with partnerships, they might have noticed the dysfunction of the group and perhaps found a way for the three of them to work together.

In contrast to Reg's partnership, let me tell you about a manufacturing company whose success story is one for all of us to learn from. Years ago, in a small town of less than nine thousand people, two individuals who identified a need and thought it would be profitable to manufacture a specialty product for aftermarket sales to a major automobile manufacturer created a company. Based on a great deal of research, planning, trial and error, and determination, they created a product that they felt deserved attention. They gave a presentation to an automobile manufacturer and received a contract to manufacture their specialty units.

The fun part is that the two men with the great idea had no manufacturing location. They were building their product in the basement of a friend's home. They had hardly spent any money on getting started, and they already had a contract with a multinational corporation. That, in my opinion, is one of the absolute best ways to start a business.

Did they just get lucky? No. They had done their research; they took a chance at sales and went all out. They knew that they only had one chance to make it with the automotive giant, so from a manufacturing perspective they knew their product needed to be perfect. There could be zero defects, so they implemented the best quality control system they could—double and triple check every unit before they sent them to the buyer.

If you have ever had the opportunity to work in a manufacturing facility, you have probably learned that this might seem excessive and not very cost efficient. Based on hours worked, the cost to make the product was much greater than what they were selling it for. So, why did they do it? For their future! They were investing in their future. They spent the time, did the planning, and knew exactly what they wanted.

The partners had great communication; they talked and planned and realized that one of them had the gift of being a great salesman, and that the other was very strong at business operations, accounting, and organization. They created an operation and procedures manual that listed their specialties, strengths, weaknesses, and job descriptions, as well as future expectations. Even though both partners were doing all of the jobs, one of them would be responsible for manufacturing and sales, and the other would manage the day-to-day operations, including banking, employees, and accounting.

Twelve years after they started, I had an opportunity to tour their manufacturing plant. It had grown from a basement corner to a major corporation with over two hundred employees. They had built the building, had a street named after the company, and paid off 75 percent of the cost to buy the property and build the huge plant. Plus, they had saved a million dollars in the bank for research and development and any future slowdowns that may occur.

This business was an incredible success, not because of the original idea and dream, but because the two partners worked hard; knew their strengths; trusted their instincts; and planned, talked, and planned some more. They had many trials and tribulations along the road as the company expanded, and nothing went along perfectly (except, of course, the quality of their products). The two partners had set the stage for victory; when they had problems, they found the advice they needed to forge ahead, and they educated themselves to ensure they met their own expectations. They saved money for the future, so they could do any required research and development and also so they could keep their employees working during any downturn in the economy.

Pointer: If you and your potential business partner take the time to create a business format or an operations and procedures manual, you will identify all sorts of strengths and shortcomings in your partnership. Overcoming these issues before starting your business will help create a successful union.

ADVICE FROM PROFESSIONALS

Often Heard Comment by New Business Owners:
*I intend to hire a manager and an accountant and just sit back
and let the cash roll in.*

Reality:
*Professional advice is invaluable, especially from lawyers
and accountants; always remember that you are ultimately
responsible for your business.*

Before signing a lease, I go to my lawyer to ensure I am not signing something that could cause me trouble in the future. Before I open a new business, I see my accountant for financial advice. Talking to these professionals allows me to be informed and comfortable with my decisions. Paying a professional for a job well done helps to secure my business future.

However, not all professionals are created equal. Before using the services of a lawyer, an accountant, or even a web designer, check their credentials or get a referral.

Buying and creating my first web page was one of the most annoying things I have ever been through as the owner and operator of a small business. I personally decided on a simple, easy to read format. Many of my target clients were new to using computers, and I didn't want to provide confusing information or make the Web site challenging to read. The other important item for me was to utilize warm and inviting colors, a very plain design, and basic fonts.

My web designer, on the other hand, had just come out of school with excellent professional training and all kinds of ideas that he insisted

I "must follow to be successful." Of course I had no understanding of the technological side of the World Wide Web, which is exactly why I hired a designer. I was not interested in how the different search engines utilized my site, and I really did not want to "sell" anything on the web; I wanted to provide information. I needed a designer to listen to my special ideas and provide me with a site that suited my needs, as well as the technology requirements. This designer came up with a very grand proposal for my web site, but it was far beyond what I desired, and the cost to implement his plans was astronomical.

I would have preferred a designer who heard what I had to say and took some time to get to know my business style before telling me the type of web site he was going to create. He was full of knowledge and had a great understanding of all the best techniques, but he would not agree to any of my ideas. As a new business owner straight out of school with only one client (me), he failed in one key aspect—clientele building. He certainly did not gain a fan in me. He didn't even try to educate me on some of his ideas; he just told me what he was going to do and expected me to follow his direction.

We argued almost daily, and I was continually frustrated by his attitude. Working with that same designer at this point in my business career would produce very different results. I would be much less tolerant and more to the point regarding my needs. But at the time, I was just starting my small business, and I wanted to keep all costs at a minimum. The web designer and I worked out a trade, which is why I endured the grief.

It was hard to get through to this guy, and I really wanted a Web site. Finally, when I was on the verge of firing him, I wrote him a letter explaining my issues. I went into great detail about the colors, the layout, and the contents. I also wrote that, "I am your customer, and if you do not agree to listen to my ideas, then I will find someone who will."

I would have loved to be a fly on the wall when the web designer read my letter because he changed immediately. He apologized for not listening to me, his customer, and promised to hear my concerns and make a serious effort to supply me with what I wanted.

Why did I let three months go by without correcting him? Because we were doing a business trade—he provided me with web services, and I provided him with a space to start up his business. The trade forced me to be more understanding than I would have been if I was paying him directly. But if he had listened to me from the beginning, he wouldn't have had to do as much work, and he would have received hundreds of referrals from me.

Once the site was complete, I really loved the simplicity of it, and so did many of my clients. However, whenever anyone asked who my designer was, I made an effort to explain how hard it had been to get what I wanted and never once did I refer his services. Even four and a half years later when he came back and asked for referrals, I chose not to write him one. Because of his bad attitude, he lost a great client who could have provided him with many referrals, which would have helped him get his business off the ground.

Our arrangement was a lesson for me and for him. We both realized how important it is to listen to our clients and to provide them with the best services possible within the parameters of our own businesses.

Something else I had to learn was that, in order to get what I wanted as a businessperson, I needed to know what it was that I wanted. The funny thing is that I wanted to hire that illusive manager that everyone dreams about—the one who could read my mind and run my business exactly as I wanted it run.

I always wondered if that person even existed until I realized that in order to find a manager that would understand and follow through with my business goals and plans, I had to train him or her first. As soon as the new manager walks in the door, before you introduce him or her to everyone else in the organization, give the new manager a binder with blank paper in it and have him or her start writing. Everything should go into this binder, including the hierarchy of the company; people's names, even who is in charge of the recycling and who has the keys to different areas; and how to use the telephones. This new manager is creating an office procedure manual that will be invaluable in a few short weeks.

Proper training and learning the details of the company will take extra time for the new manager in the initial stages but it will be well worth the effort in the long run. And never assume that the new manager will automatically know what to do; show him or her, teach him or her, and ensure that he or she knows what you want. Add to the binder all existing documentation that you have for your business. As you and the manager go through the documentation, you will probably notice items that need to be updated, organized, or thrown out. This is a very effective exercise in organizing your business and ensuring that the manager is onboard with the rest of the organization. Ensure that he or she writes down everything you teach, as well as any questions that arise; then review the office procedural manual with your manager regularly, until you have achieved a complete document that explains your business. After that, have the manager schedule time each month to keep it up-to-date for future employees and customers.

Should you be wondering why a procedure manual is under the chapter entitled "Advice from Professionals"? Let me tell you this: A current procedures manual is one very useful tool in operating a business. For new employees, it is like having a professional adviser or manager at their fingertips.

One of my clients, Ellee, adds all information that she learns from her lawyer and her accountant into her manual. When new employees ask questions, she always says, "Check the book; once you find the answer, come and discuss it with me." Ellee runs a small photography studio and, in the spring, gets so busy that she often uses the services of temporary staffing. The manual is a lifesaver that allows her to minimize her time training temporary staff.

Ellee laughs as she describes herself as a very intense, anal, high-maintenance person who cannot stand incompetent employees. I guess if a manual could work for someone with those credentials, it would probably work for just about anyone.

In all seriousness though, even if you are the smartest person you know, it doesn't hurt to get advice. You may hear an idea that you never thought of, or you may actually learn something. And the most exciting part is the professional who helps you might actually save your butt.

Pointer: Your web designer, lawyer, and accountant will not know everything about your business; they work with the information you give them. Ask enough questions until you understand what your advisers are saying, especially if your instincts are nagging at you. Mistakes are made in every profession.

TRUSTING YOUR
COMMERCIAL LEASE

Often Heard Comment by New Business Owners:
*There are lease laws put in place by the government, so you really
do not need to read the entire lease agreement.*

Reality:
*A lease is a legal document; there is nothing more to know.
If you sign it, you are responsible for it, so always take lease
documentation seriously.*

One of the smartest things new business owners can do is to go over
their business lease with a lawyer *before* they sign it. Leases are signed
on a daily basis by businesses of all sorts so being informed about
leasing before you sign will help increase your chance of future business
success.

Have you ever heard the term *triple net* and wondered what it
means? Another lease term is *gross* lease, and one or the other will apply
to the commercial lease you sign with your landlord. With a gross
lease, the tenant generally makes one regular, monthly payment, which
includes all costs for the space. A lease with triple net generally has the
tenant paying for the rent as well as additional items, such as property
taxes, maintenance, and insurance, often referred to as "extra rent."
The amount charged for triple net is generally paid on a monthly basis;
however, at the end of the year, the costs for the entire building/space
are calculated and divided by the square footage of each space. If the
monthly payments for all extra rents do not cover the yearly bills, then

a charge is put back to each of the tenants based on the square footage of their lease.

Trusting blindly that your lease is in your best interest is not the way to commence business. Make it a priority to read your lease before you sign it—all of it. Ask questions of the landlord to ensure you understand what you are signing. Do you agree with everything? Are you signing a personal agreement or indemnity? What if your company does not make it past the first year and you have signed a three-year lease? Who is responsible for paying that lease for the remaining two years?

Leases are legal documents and should be taken very seriously. The learning curve never ends. I have been working in business for many years, which is just about long enough to get cocky and overconfident. I have received many compliments about my business skills, which pad my ego, but I still must be diligent in my procedures.

About four years after I began my business, I opened a second one. It seemed like a natural progression, and I was very excited about the prospect and worked diligently on two successful businesses. Then one day, I received a serious wake-up call. My bookkeeper phoned to tell me for the second time, (she tried to tell me the month before but I didn't believe her) that I had three thousand nine hundred dollars in outstanding receivables from the damage deposit and first month's lease of a company we'll call Freddie's Freight Company. I argued with her, explaining that she must have made a mistake, as I always double-checked my receivables. We spent three hours going over the books and analyzing the entries so I could prove she was wrong.

We went back to where the error had all started, seven months prior when Freddie's had hired my company to provide regular administration and office space. Freddie's was a very large company with hundreds of employees and a great reputation, so I was thrilled to gain the company as a client. I was unconcerned when Freddie's first deposit check came back from the bank with nonsufficient funds because someone from the company explained that they had switched bank accounts and the bank had made an error. A new check would be issued, and I would have it in a week.

It took two full weeks for that replacement check to arrive, and much to my surprise, it bounced as well. Extremely frustrated, I contacted one of the owners of the company, who assured me everything would be taken care of and another new check would be issued right away.

In the meantime, I was extremely busy training two new employees and preparing for a weeklong conference out of town. I began to realize that one of my new employees, who we'll call Betty, was not a good fit and would need to be let go. Due to the fact that I would be leaving in a couple of days, I decided to keep her working until I returned from my trip.

The importance of making a decision never ceases to amaze me; almost immediately, Betty started to go downhill faster than before, and I hadn't even told her she was going to be let go. Her performance went from bad to worse, and I walked into the office during her lunch to find that she had left and had not locked the front door.

The next day, I brought in a very trusted and long-term employee and had her work with Betty for the day to learn all of the passwords, codes, and procedures. I also informed Betty that she would no longer be employed by the organization.

Again I was hit with a large wake-up call. Do you ever wonder why businesspeople walk fired employees immediately out the door without allowing them any time to say good-bye? Not doing so allows the fired employee to get angry and try to get back at the employer.

I never thought it would happen to me, as I always made an effort to be upfront and honest with my employees, and I usually received the same in return. But such was not the case this time. During that day, Betty managed to delete our entire operations and procedures manual from the computer, and she also changed all of the passwords and deleted the majority of the work she had done over the past month. Normally, this would not be a big issue due to our diligent computer backups, but we had just put in a new computer system one month earlier and were waiting for our tech guy to set up the backup program. We had no backups.

I contacted the police and learned of my rights, then phoned Betty at home and informed her I wanted to have her charged with theft. She pretended she didn't know what I was talking about, but the very next day we received a CD with all of the deleted information. I was lucky.

The conference started that week, and so off I went, feeling very stressed and hoping all would be well back at home. Upon returning, I made a procedural change to ensure that all accounts receivable would be dealt with efficiently.

Remember the bounced checks from Freddie's Freight? Well, by this time I had forgotten all about their series of NSF checks, and their regular rent checks had begun to arrive in a timely manner. Approximately three months later, though, the checks stopped coming, and I learned that Freddie's had gone bankrupt, and many of their employees had not been paid for an entire month. Personally, I was not worried as I was convinced that I had their security deposit, so I wouldn't lose out.

Business was going according to plan, until the dreaded phone call from my bookkeeper. I had been ripped off months previously by Freddie's and had not even noticed. I had no means of getting the money back because the company no longer existed. I never did get my three thousand nine hundred-dollar damage deposit and first month's lease payment.

Emotionally, this error hit me hard, and it took weeks to get over the loss of income. That was my personal income lost, not anyone else's. I had screwed up by not following through. I had to admit that I'd learned a great lesson about time management, people management, and personal management. I also began to realize that I had too much work on my hands and, short of working eighty hours per week, I would never get ahead.

Then suddenly I realized that my ego was getting the better of me. It was time to go back to the basics of my business, complete my operations and procedures manual, and get my companies running properly. I went over procedures with a fine-toothed comb. I left no stone unturned and was diligent in my operations. It was time to standardize all of my business procedures to ensure all functions were taken care of on a daily basis.

Updating my operations and procedures manual on a regular basis has allowed me to take *me* out of my business. It might sound odd that I would try to standardize the procedures in my small business, and some may actually think that doing so is a waste of time. Fortunately, I knew better. When payments and leases from my customers came due, I would know exactly how to handle them.

When a good friend named Dale asked for leasing advice, I was all ears and excited to help. The following is what Dale and I both learned about renewing a commercial lease. Dale had notified his landlord that he wished to continue leasing the space he was in and was interested in renewing his lease. The landlord informed Dale that he was no longer able to renew his lease; however, he would definitely be able to sign an entirely new one. Doesn't that sound like two different ways of saying the same thing? What could be different about renewing his existing lease versus signing an entirely new lease with the same old landlords? Well, I am here to tell you that they are not the same thing.

The new lease the landlords offered increased Dale's monthly payments by 39 percent. They had changed over to a triple net lease and, using that as an excuse, increased Dale's payment by one thousand nine hundred seventy dollars per month. No wonder Dale wanted advice.

Dale was an excellent tenant who had paid his rent on time every month for the past five and a half years. He always tried to help other companies in the building and was the type of tenant that every landlord dreams of. After talking with other landlords in the industry to see if they had any ideas on how to negotiate his lease, Dale wrote a letter to his landlord, explaining that he was a small company and that a 39 percent lease increase was something that could potentially put his business into bankruptcy; he could lose everything. He also gave examples of other buildings that offered more reasonable rents than the one offered to him. His hopes were dashed when the landlord simply wrote back that the commercial market was booming, that they were treating him as fairly as possible, and that the rental increase was something that the local market would bare. They also informed Dale that, if he wished, he could move his business elsewhere. For Dale, location was one of the main features that attracted his clients. He had no choice but to accept the increase.

Dale had expected and planned for an increase in his lease. As he was a good tenant and a good person, he automatically assumed that his landlords would be fair in their offering and expected nothing more than a 15 or 20 percent increase.

With this 39 percent lease increase, Dale was forced to make major cutbacks in business, and at the same time, he had to increase the price of all the services he offered. Naturally, this did have a large impact on his customer base. He lost some of his customers at this time and learned that money in the bank for hard times is an absolute necessity.

Pointer: Residential leases are regulated by government set standards, whereas commercial leases are based on the actual documentation (your lease) set out by each and every business. Before going into any lease negotiations, look around for other spots to open your business. Negotiations are far more effective when you have another possible location in mind, even if the second location isn't exactly perfect.

GOOD BOUNDARIES KEEP QUALITY CUSTOMERS

Often Heard Comment by New Business Owners:
I can provide the right product at the right price with the best service possible, and I should have no problems with my customers.

Reality:
All customers are not all created equal. Some make your job easy while others will have constant demands. Every customer is different, and there is truly no specific system to keep them all happy, but using common sense helps.

Good boundaries help keep good, quality customers, but the question most businesses face is this: Where should the boundaries be drawn? Sometimes good clientele think they can get away with things such as paying their bills late, not showing up on time for meetings, bouncing checks, or ignoring your calls just because they think they can. Are they still good customers? Do you still want to keep them? The answer is usually yes you do want to keep them, but you also want them to treat you with the respect you deserve.

So, how do you get what you need without making the client mad? Honest and true communication is usually the best method for keeping business relationships intact. Try to stop unacceptable behavior before it makes you angry enough to blow up. Be firm but kind and explain to your customer that his or her actions are affecting your business. Most customers will be surprised and even a little bit embarrassed, as they probably did not do anything intentional.

My friend, Cole, has a great method of fixing customers who have gone bad. He doesn't allow them to go bad. He has a complete new customer package that he goes over with every client before allowing them to sign a contract. In his industry, this method is unheard of, but I believe that is why Cole has done so well. He has been operating his property management company for over twenty-five years, with success beyond belief. He is five short years away from early retirement and handing his business down to his daughter. Cole wants the next five years of his life to be profitable, fun, and low on stress. He will most likely produce exactly what he desires because he has set his business up to suit his needs.

Reflecting on the past twenty-five years, Cole is proud of his accomplishments. He went through many tough times and almost lost the business after the first three years. Right at that point, Cole knew things had to change. He wanted to keep his business. He loved being the boss and making decisions, but he realized that he needed a format in place to ensure that his employees understood his business concept and were able to convey his ideas to the customers. Why did he need this format in place? Because Cole is a friendly, fun loving businessman who made decisions on the fly and often forgot to communicate changes to his employees.

He called a staff meeting and hired a coach to take notes and help make suggestions for running a smoother operation. His employees felt that he was squandering essential finances on a business coach when all he needed to do was ask their opinions. Little did they realize that each time he asked for their input, an argument ensued as to who was utilizing the best procedures.

The business coach, who was recommended by a trusted colleague, was exactly what Cole needed to turn the operation around and make it profitable. The coach started with an eight page how-to manual that provided general property management rules based on existing companies in the field. Next, he met with each employee individually to get feedback on the manual and then sat down with Cole for the final touches. When the coach was complete, he handed Cole and his employees a professional tool—a twenty-page manual that captured the essence of the business.

At this point Cole could have paid the coach for a job well done and sent him on his way but he wanted to ensure that the changes were implemented and adhered to. He kept the coach on for another month, even though he was still financially strapped. During that month, Cole's company began to change, and so did Cole and his employees. It wasn't long before the customers started to see the difference, which had an effect on the bottom line. Cole was thrilled, as his venture slowly but surely became successful. He contracted the coach to come in once per month to help maintain the growth and keep the lines of communication open.

I talked with Cole and learned that, in his opinion, the best thing he learned from the business coach was to put plans in place to ensure that all customers fully understand their responsibilities before any contracts were signed. Creating his new tenant package took hours of work, but in the long run, it saved him years of aggravation with uninformed clients.

A great way to keep good customers is by keeping clear boundaries. Try to keep important details to yourself. Some of you may be thinking, *I keep everything to myself* (which on its own level is not exactly great either), but it is important to learn when to be open and honest and when to keep quiet. It is easy to make friends with clients; they tell you their stories and you may want to reciprocate to form a bond. It feels good to have a relationship with a client—unless he or she forgets to be respectful of your time and business.

Communication is one business tool that should never be underrated. Many of us think that our customers should already know what we are thinking, but remember that good, consistent communication is one of the best ways to keep your customers happy. Not knowing or guessing often leads to negative thinking.

Deal with problems head on and do your best to come up with a solution that solves everyone's issues, but always remember to not compromise your business ethics or change your plans for the whims of an individual customer.

I had a customer named Gerald, who was a nasty customer and seemed to bring everyone down. He was an employee of an international computer organization and a manager of two people. When he was in the office, his one and only goal was to make money for the company without any consideration for the well-being of anyone else around him. His standards were very high. He was always immaculately dressed, his shoes were as shiny as his car, and he very seldom smiled. He complained about the telephone system, the noise, the other people and even the flavor of the coffee. I made a serious effort to make him happy, as his company was paying approximately 10 percent of my income. I spent money on soundproofing, invested in a high-end telephone system, and changed the coffee, and still Gerald found things to complain about. He was a very aggressive person, and everyone was quiet when he came around for fear of upsetting him. One Christmas, we had an in-office party that he refused to attend and would not allow his employees attend. The Christmas party lasted for two hours, and once again, he was angry that we were all talking too loud.

My goal was to run a calm and friendly business. Even though his company paid their bills on time and treated me with respect, Gerald was a problem, and after a year or so, I realized that I could no longer tolerate his behavior. I stopped jumping at all of his concerns and concentrated my efforts on making my other customers happy. It took about two weeks before Gerald got really angry and told me that I had better start making changes, or he would move out. I did not want to lose the income that his company was providing, yet it was necessary to set my boundaries and tell him I would not be making any more changes to suit his needs.

When Gerald finally moved out about two months later, I was relieved and so was everyone else in the office. My fear about losing a lucrative customer was unnecessary, as the income from Gerald's company was replaced almost immediately, and I felt no financial differences. A momentary setback was a chance I had to take to keep my business priorities in order. I learned that angry people would come and go, but my morals and business goals were the attributes that set me apart from other businesses.

Pointer: Creating good, solid rules about price increases, discounts, referrals, and freebies before you open your business will help to ensure that all of your customers are treated fairly.

GET IT RUNNING AND SELL IT

Often Heard Comment by New Business Owners:
*I will open a business, get it up and running, and then sell it for
a huge profit.*

Reality:
*Quick, profitable sales have been the fates of a few fortunate
enterprises, but more realistically, selling your business doesn't
happen that easily. A potential buyer will require a substantial
amount of history to prove to a financier that the business is
profitable.*

One of the best parts of owning a business is that you can sell it! That's
what I have always heard, but the reality isn't quite all it is touted to be.
A business with assets, such as trucks owned by a delivery company or
land owned by a corporation, will always have value in the eyes of the
banking industry; however, a business based solely on services does not
hold the same merit.

Sarah was the owner of an extremely successful leasing company
that had been in existence for sixteen years. She was a self-made woman
with time for holidays every six months, a cottage on the lake, and a
very beautiful home. Many businesspeople looked at Sarah with envy,
as she seemed to have it all.

When she decided to sell her business, she discovered, much to
her dismay, that the banks felt that the company was worth only a
third of the yearly profit because she had no direct assets, with the
exception of basic office equipment and six months left on her current
lease agreement with her landlord. The banks felt that the "goodwill"

Sarah had created over the past sixteen years might end when Sarah left the company. Without Sarah at the helm, the business had very little value because she was the reason the business worked so well. She had relationships with the customers and brokers, who knew that she was an excellent businesswoman, and they continued to do business with her year after year.

She also had a terrific computer system and database that allowed her to keep data on clients virtually indefinitely. The system was perfectly up-to-date and was part of the agreement for sale. The database, which was only information, was an asset in itself, but how could one place a value on it? If a purchaser had no prior knowledge of the industry, the database would be virtually useless; however, to an existing company in the leasing industry, that same database would be invaluable.

For Sarah to be able to sell her business, it was necessary to find someone who could see the value with no need to turn to a bank for funding. She accepted the first offer because she felt it was one she could not refuse, and the only condition from the buyers was that their accountants needed to review three years of the business books. She was very excited, as the offer was close to her asking price, and she knew that her business books were up-to-date and accurate.

Much to Sarah's surprise, the buyers found all kinds of items to complain about in the books. During the next forty-five days, the buyers had reduced their offer by two-thirds, and Sarah had spent over twenty thousand dollars on legal fees. Extremely stressed and frustrated, Sarah learned from her advisers that this type of thing happens very often when people try to sell a business and that she had very little recourse.

Also, as the potential purchaser was looking over the books, Sarah's two employees got wind of the sale, and they both quit. One of the employees had been with Sarah since the inception of the business, so the blow was not only to the business operations, but, emotionally, Sarah had a hard time dealing with the loss.

Another associate was very interested in purchasing Sarah's business, so she started to work out a deal with him. The deal wasn't what Sarah wanted, but it was certainly better than nothing. Sarah would fund this associate in business for one year and also provide training for three months. It wasn't the best-case scenario, as it was a very risky venture for Sarah, but it was one of the most workable options. Also, Sarah would still get what she was asking for, but it would take extra time for everything to work out.

Just as Sarah was ready to seal the deal, she learned that she really wasn't legally able to sell because she had accepted the original offer, and there was a time period clause in the contract—the one that had already cost her twenty thousand dollars in legal fees. Short of going to court, there was nothing she could do except wait. She had to continue to run the business for a longer period of time before she would be able to sell—so much for her early retirement.

Perhaps there were ways that Sarah could have done things differently, but she felt the fight would cost far too much money and was not worth it.

The best part of Sarah's story is she now has part of her dream coming true, with the help of her husband; she packed up her business and moved it to an office in her home. This decision changed the dynamics of her business, as there was no professional office to see clients in, but most of them were from out of town anyway. Fortunately, working from home has reduced Sarah's overhead and increased her profits. She has fired a couple of clients who were hard to deal with, and she call forwards her telephone to a part-time employee when she wants to take a holiday. She will retire sooner or later and probably sell the business to her part-time employee, who already understands its value.

Sarah is not the only person with a problem selling a business, as we shall hear about in the account of Aderly. Aderly owned and operated a small, retail store in a busy part of Vancouver. She was a warm and friendly person, thrilled to open a business and take charge of her future. Always dreaming of running a little shop that provided the kind of service that was important to Aderly, she took the plunge. She had many goals and aspirations, but her main objective was to attract the kind people that she would have as friends.

Most friends of hers supported her decision to open a business, but as often happens, some of the people she knew pressed her with negative news about the economy and took every opportunity to try to convince Aderly that she had made a bad decision. Aderly had such a wonderful feeling of success; when one of her negative friends asked for a job, all Aderly could think was, *not a chance*, but instead, she politely said that she did not require any help at that time.

She ran a very lucrative business because she spent time talking to her customers, learning their needs, and giving them what they wanted. Her slow, relaxed style limited her customer base, but because she targeted a specific clientele, she was able to qualify her customers before they came in the door. This she sensed was the opposite of the big-box stores, which seemed to aim their products and marketing at that "mythical, average person" to maximize their sales.

Five years after she began her business, she decided to sell it for a profit and move onto bigger and better things. She told some of her current clients that she was selling and one of them was very excited to see the books and perhaps buy the business.

Everything had fallen into place just as Aderly had expected it would; all she had to do was sign a new lease with the landlord. The lease was coming due within six months, so she contacted her landlord and began the new lease negotiation process. When Aderly had first opened her business, there had been a great deal of retail space available throughout the city, and she'd been able to negotiate an amazing deal. At Aderly's cost, she would do all of her own lease improvements (with the help of her family), and at that time, the landlord had given her three months rent/lease-free to entice her to sign for five years.

Five years later, Aderly was shocked to learn how much had changed since she'd begun her business. She felt like she had just been punched in the stomach when her landlord came back with a 47 percent overall increase. It was unthinkable. She was horrified. How could she afford it; it would never work. She would never be able to sell the business. She would probably lose everything, all because her landlord was greedy. At least these were the thoughts playing over and over again in her mind. She was devastated.

After about two weeks of complete and utter self-pity, Aderly decided to fight back. She got advice from associates who had been in the business for a long time and proved to the landlord that the astronomical increase was unacceptable. All the details were listed in her letter to the landlord, as she requested that her lease be reviewed and perhaps a much more affordable conclusion be reached.

And, once again, the landlord came back to Aderly with the wrong answer—or, should I say, the wrong answer according to Aderly? Her landlord felt that the increase was acceptable and that the current market could bear the cost.

Wow, that was sooo not the answer that Aderly was looking for. Luckily, Aderly had an opportunity to see her business coach and came out feeling once again that she was in control of her venture. She went back to her original business plan and decided that her little retail shop could still be a great moneymaker, but she needed to make some changes.

Even though Aderly was in the process of negotiating the sale of her business with one of her clients, they had not put anything in writing at this point, so she chose to stop the sale. This was a very tough decision for Aderly because she didn't want to hurt her prospective buyer/client, who was about to present an offer. As Aderly knew the value and potential value of the business, she was not ready to accept too low an offer, so she stopped it before it happened.

Aderly then scrutinized all of her products and processes to find areas that she could modify, such as business hours, products, prices, suppliers, revising her advertising campaign, and perhaps, starting a Web site to increase sales. It was astounding how accepting Aderly had become with her suppliers over the past five years. Instead of searching and researching the best possible product for the best possible price, as she had done in the beginning, Aderly had allowed her suppliers to dictate the prices. This was the first area to change. She explained to her existing suppliers the situation she was in and asked them to help out; plus, she found new suppliers and went out for proposals. Within two weeks, Aderly had reduced her product costs by 11 percent, which kind of made her mad, as she could have been making better money all along, had she not become complacent.

The next step was to analyze the business hours. She found that the first hour of business each day was spent doing books and puttering around the store. Very few customers actually came in the store, so why was she wasting her time and money during that hour, not to mention the part-time employee who she paid to work that extra hour two times per week.

Within one month, Aderly had increased her profits dramatically. Was she surprised? Not really! She was the one with the dream and the knowledge to carry her dream forward. Sure that was five years ago, but suddenly Aderly was enjoying going to work and was having second thoughts about selling. Maybe she could keep her little shop after all; it was bringing in good money.

The last time I talked to Aderly, she was very excited about launching her new Web site, product line, and advertising campaign. The person who was interested in buying Aderly's business was very impressed with everything that Aderly had accomplished and had asked if she could open a franchise of the little shop.

Aderly had plenty of work to do over the next while and having the experiences of the past ups and downs, encouraged her to grow her business in ways she had never thought imaginable.

Pointer: If you ever find yourself bored and complacent about your business, talk to a business coach, get some input from kind friends, or just look at your products and processes. What could you do differently that would bring your enthusiasm back?

IT *IS* ALL ABOUT YOU

Often Heard Comment by New Business Owners:
*Running my own business will be so great—I can set my own
hours and be my own boss.*

Reality:
*Yes, you can set your own hours and become your own boss, but
remember, you must take full responsibility for your investment.*

All my life, I wanted to own a business. I had no idea what type, so I
tried all of the low-cost, moneymaking schemes available. Multilevel
marketing was always touted to be the easy money maker, so I gave
it a try. I sold pantyhose, jewelry, plastic food containers, electronics,
and even really great products that were the basis of a unique religious
group. All of the schemes worked to some degree and I had some
success with them all.

The biggest problem I had was following someone else's rules.
I chose to believe in what other people were telling me, rather than
discovering my own beliefs. Needless to say, all of these schemes left me
feeling embarrassed. I had talked many of my friends into following
me, made a couple of enemies, and tried to do what each "multilevel
marketing company" told me to do.

One friend, who had brought me into a multilevel marketing
scheme, was shocked when I decided to quit. I loved the products
and the business idea that had originally been presented, but as time
went by, I began to realize that the principals of the company had
misrepresented themselves. They had no desire to sell products; their
goal was to collect people they could help, people that they could train

71

in their way of life, and people who would then go on to teach their beliefs. When I explained to my friend why I was quitting, she said she felt the same way but had to stick with the business because she had no other choice. It was my turn to be shocked.

Please do not misunderstand me; multilevel marketing has been very profitable for many organizations and individuals, just not me. I personally need to be involved in the decision making of any business I own. I will not blindly adopt others' opinions and plans as if they were my own. I wanted my friend to understand that, as individuals, we live our lives and create business ideas from our thoughts, how we know the world, and what we believe we see. We are exactly who we think we are, and if we wish to change, we will need to change our thoughts as well.

I was working as a manager in one of the multilevel companies mentioned above. I had my own office with lots of windows, and I enjoyed selling inventory to all the "new starts" coming into the business. With all my heart, I believed in the products I was selling, and I wanted to own part of the company.

One day, the president asked me if I was interested in becoming a partner; all I had to do was invest five thousand dollars, and I was in. Wow, little ole me was going to own a business. I went to a friend and borrowed the five thousand dollars and promptly took it to the president of the company. I sat back in my office smiling at myself because now I was a business owner.

Not once did I ever ask to see the company books; nor did I look into how the corporation was structured. Was I truly a business partner? Within about three months, the truth became apparent. The company needed my money to survive, and five thousand dollars could only get us so far.

I started asking questions about the business operations, accounts receivable, and cash flow, and suddenly the president informed me that I was far too negative, and she didn't really want me around the business anymore. So I quit.

What was I thinking? I was young and naive and had just learned a big lesson in life. Money is a precious commodity, and I had just thrown away five thousand dollars, and it wasn't even mine. I still had to pay my friend back, with interest, and for what? So I could have bragging rights and tell my friends that I was part owner of a corporation.

When I look back to that time, I realize that I had no forward thinking; nor did I have a true opinion of my own. Oh, maybe I thought I was an open-minded professional, but in reality, I was personally living an accumulation of my past, and I continued to create the same familiar situations that I knew and understood.

Obviously, I wasn't born with my current level of confidence in business; I have learned the hard way, through trial and error. My parents owned and operated small businesses, so it seemed obvious to me that I would run my own operation, even if I didn't know what I was doing.

Just after I lost the five thousand dollars in my not-so-great investment, my life was flipped upside down with a divorce, a car accident, and bad health, and then I ran out of money. I will spare you the details of being sick, but needless to say I didn't even realize how sick I was or how badly I needed to stay home and rest. I found a job as a salesperson and had little naps in my car between my appointments. I dragged myself out of bed, so I could drive like an angry maniac to the 7:00 a.m. sales "rah-rah" sessions. Although these sessions were quite annoying at the time, I learned a great deal about selling, which is the main ingredient in my business success. I learned how to cold call. I did so much cold calling that it stopped scaring me, and I got really good at it.

Operating a business is far easier when you can walk into another business, introduce yourself, and have a true, honest conversation about what you do.

If this is terrifying, try to do it in little steps, such as visiting one business per day in your building. Tell yourself that you will just talk to one business, just one. Then visit one business, and no matter the results, give yourself a pat on the back for a job well done. That one business owner now knows what you do, and he or she may tell a friend or two. Truly, it is not that hard, and it's much cheaper than advertising. The next day, do it again, and then do it every day for five days.

Once you've done this, you need to take a break and reflect on the fact that you just completed five cold calls, which is often five more calls than most other start-up businesses ever do. Congratulations!

The next day, you need to talk to two more business. You can even do it while you are shopping or visiting a friend or walking through the mall. Make it easy and only do two. Then do two more a day for five days.

Here is the fun part: We are never going to increase the cold calls to more than two per day or ten per week. Eventually, you will find that talking to other businesses about what you do will become natural. Like it should be! Always remember to listen when you do cold calls because you may learn something or get a great idea or make a new business contact.

This type of business networking can make your business work when others fail. It gives you a leg up over the competition and adds to your local knowledge. You might even gain some valuable advice; of course, you may get some crummy advice, but that just comes with the territory. Be open to what you hear and, before you implement new ideas, ensure that you fully research them.

Owning my small businesses, I have received a great deal of advice over the years from loving people who all meant well but I often wonder whom was that advice intended? Probably the person giving the advice because none of those advisors had any idea what my thoughts and future plans were. I heard many things such as:

- Lots of businesses fail, and yours does not sound very exciting.
- You can have such a great job; don't open a business— what if it doesn't work?
- Are you sure you are making the right decision? I'm not sure about that business.
- My brother had a business like that, and he didn't make any money. I wouldn't do it if I were you.
- If you didn't work so many hours, you'd feel better.
- If you worked harder, you'd feel better.
- You should charge more for your products.
- Your prices are too high.

And on and on this list goes. In the early stages of business ownership, I would receive all kinds of "advice" and wonder if I was doing the wrong thing, but as time went on, I realized that some of my decisions were excellent, and some were a little off. However, the only person who really needed to be happy about the results was me—me, just me!

When I really trust myself and make sound decisions based on research that is solidified by my gut instincts, they are usually the right choices. Maybe they turn out different than my expectations, but often I learn some type of lesson in the process. As business owners, we need to understand the importance of trusting in ourselves, even if we have heard that we don't know what we are doing. Because life is all about us! If we are happy, we will exude happiness, which will spill over to other people and make the world around us a better place; and customers will want to do business with us.

As we go through our adult lives, it is our responsibility to learn what is right and what is wrong, and it is our turn to make rules to live by. Where do we start? What rules are important? This topic can be and has been debated for years, so as a starting place I will let you in on some of my personal rules.

That the average person needs to have eight hours of sleep per day to keep the body functioning at its best has been promoted by the media for years. But, as I have stated earlier no one knows me like I do; those statistics are for the average, the median, and the mean—not me. Eight hours sleep is what the average person requires and I am not average. Eight hours of sleep leaves me somewhat rested, a little cranky, and a little slow at making decisions. Because my body prefers more than eight hours sleep per night, as I have sleep apnea.

Sleep is an all-important commodity for small business owners. Lack of sleep results in being stressed out and often leads to a hatred of the business that should bring so much happiness. When a business relies solely on one person's health to succeed, that one person should take the time to ensure he or she doesn't burn out. Planning and running a business is very exciting, and often an individual's limitations are ignored for the sake of the enterprise. This is a bad direction to take because, at some point, you will end up so exhausted that you actually make mistakes and bad decisions.

Again I'm referring to the importance of trust and instincts to your small business—take care of your health, so you'll have the energy to run your business. Always be kind to yourself. Keep your thoughts as positive as possible and treat others as you would like to be treated.

I know a really fun guy named Adam who is a successful truck driver and loves being out on the open road driving long distances. He also understands the importance of instincts and positive self-talk because he spent a large part of his life doing jobs that left him feeling miserable, not to mention that the constant repetitive motions of these jobs left his joints and muscles in pain. Adam worked in two different factories doing monotonous jobs that did not suit him. The jobs allowed him plenty of time to think and, unfortunately for Adam, the majority of his thoughts were negative ones. One day, a friend gave him a book [3]by Norman Vincent Peale called *Positive Imaging: The Powerful Way to Change Your Life* and his life began to change. He realized that the more he told himself how miserable he was, the more miserable he became. He also learned that, as he was complaining about his job, his employer, and his fellow employees, he was really just making himself more depressed. It was a vicious cycle.

Once Adam learned about positive imaging, he began listening to his thoughts and wanted to change his life. He made up a mantra that he could use whenever negative thoughts came into his life. His mantra was this: My life is filled with happiness as I work in a career that I love. Adam said this mantra over and over again until he started to believe it. He began smiling more often and always tried to do things that would make him happy. At work, he began to get along better with his co-workers because he understood how they felt. The owner of the company noticed the change and offered Adam a new job in the company. The job would be delivering products to customers thousands of miles away in a Class 8 truck.

Of course Adam accepted the position, but with a twist. Adam's twist was that he wanted to set the job up as a business and purchase his own truck. That way he would have an asset to sell in the future, should he ever decide to quit. Adam wrote up a plan detailing the costs of fuel, maintenance, repairs, and bookkeeping; plus, he also detailed the amount of income he required and presented it to the owner of the company. The owner also felt it was a good opportunity, as it would reduce his liabilities, so he agreed to the plan and even financed Adam's new truck.

A mere ten months passed from the time Adam began to use positive self-talk at his job to when he started his long-haul trucking company. Years later, Adam is still enjoying his career and always has a positive mantra. He loves his work so much he says he never wants to retire. Not wanting to burst his happiness bubble, I didn't mention that he should start planning for retirement.

Retirement, why would I bring that up when a business is just getting started? I think an important step in planning your business is preparing ahead for retirement or illness. It doesn't matter what age you are, an illness can stop you and your business from moving forward, and bankruptcy is a horrible thought for your future. Financial planners and accountants can be very helpful in this exercise; however, there are many retirement planning techniques available.

So the question often arises: How can a person change his or her lifestyle and start planning for the future when he or she has no extra money to work with? What good is it to plan for your financial future if you can barely make ends meet?

It's surprising how a little cash in the bank can help you feel confident. I had no extra money, and neither did my business when I started to save, but I put away ten dollars each month—I didn't even notice a difference. That doesn't seem like much, but one month I had a bit of extra money, and I put it in the bank. Slowly but surely, the most amazing thing happened. That small amount of money in the bank helped me to attract more money. I had always heard that, to be able to attract prosperity, I needed to think differently than before, and having money in the bank helped me to do that.

I knew the money was there if I ever needed it, but I never did. In fact, I kept adding more and more and more. I saved enough to have an extra lease payment in the bank. It felt great.

Many of us small business owners feel anxious and worried at different stages of our business careers. We may be looking at a friend, a workmate, or even another business owner and wishing we had it all together like he or she does. Well, guess what? Many times, those people are looking at us and thinking the exact same thing. Remember the old saying: The grass is always greener on the other side of the fence. It doesn't just apply to cows; it applies to each and every one of us. If only we had more money, more time, a business that made more money, better health, a nicer house, or even a better spouse—just like the business or family down the street. They seem to have everything.

I talked about Sarah selling her business in an earlier chapter and having a horrible experience doing it, which leads to how I reduced my workload. I decided to sell one of my newly opened businesses. To me, it sounded like a great idea. The business was sound and profitable and, with the operations and procedures manual in place, a new owner would have no problem learning the business. I would make some money selling the place, and the new owners would have a great plan to work with. It was a win-win situation.

Wrong again. You may be thinking that, with the lessons I had learned so far, I should have been a pretty strong and intelligent businessperson making great decisions and moving forward, but I had only just begun to learn.

I felt that I had set up a strong, organized, and efficient business. I was proud of my success and thought that the new business owner felt the same way. Perhaps my ego was in the way again, or maybe the problem was a lack of communication; whatever the case, within one month of selling the business, I realized that the new people did not think the way I did. They wanted to do business the "easy way" and asked that I stop coming by to train them. They wanted to use my employees and pay them "under the table," which, they said, was the best way to save money. I was flabbergasted. Were they nuts? This was a real business operating according to the laws of the government. Procedures were listed in a complete Operations and Procedures Manual. There was no guesswork to this business. It should have been cut-and-dried—easy to run and easy to make money.

But, like I said, the new people did not think like me. They couldn't see that I had set the business up in a manner to ensure that everything would run smoothly; nor could they see that the rules would help the business be successful and continue to grow. All they could see was that I was trying to tell them what to do. They said I was trying to control them, and they were not going to allow me to. What a shock for me: I thought I was being helpful

It took a long time to learn how to let the business go and grow in a different direction than I had planned. My hope now is that the new owners will be successful with their business (even if they are not doing it my way) and that their future is as bright as mine.

I am now certain that the new owners of the business know something that I do not. They know themselves and know how they want to run their business. Hopefully, they take the time to hear their clients' needs and offer solutions. But, more importantly, I hope they are true to themselves and do whatever it takes to make the business work. It truly all comes down to trust and instincts.

Pointer: Do what works, but don't bury your head in the sand and pretend that everything is OK. If your guts are telling you there is a problem, then there probably is. Should you address it even if it might it wreck the business? I say "Yes". If you don't deal with the issues, they will continue to compound and possibly drag down the business anyway.

[3]Vincent Peale, Norman, A Fawcett Columbine Book, Published by Ballantine Books, Copy write 1982 by Norman Vincent Peale

HOW TO PLAN YOUR BUSINESS IN TEN NOT-SO-EASY STEPS

1. Do your business research

a. Learn and fully understand the product you wish to sell, whether it is an actual tangible item or a service.

b. Talk to professionals, such as lawyers, accountants, and financial planners.

c. Find other business owners who you can speak to for moral support or direction.

d. Research the organization(s) that will provide your products. Have they been in business long, or are they just starting up as well?

e. Source another supplier for your products, in case anything happens to your current provider.

2. Do your personal research

a. What kind of things do you truly like to do?

b. Does your family support you? Do they realize how much time you will devote to this project?

c. Can you involve your family and help them learn something new?

d. Do you like to do paperwork, or would your time be better spent doing sales?

e. Do you have the confidence to stick to your convictions?

f. Do you like doing sales or will you need a salesperson?

3. Look into extra learning

a.   You may not have the time or the inclination to get a degree, but many local schools and colleges provide short courses that would save you a ton of time on your business.

b.   Take a short bookkeeping course.

c.   Learn whether a partnership would work for your type of business.

d.   Take the time to read some business books. I personally recommend 4 *The eMyth: Why Most Small Businesses Don't Work and What to Do about It* by Michael Gerber.

e.   Internet research is free. Go for it; learn what your competitors do, where they are, and who they are.

4. Learn the financial requirements of the business

a.   Should you take out a loan or use your credit cards?

b.   Do you have a nest egg that you would like to spend to get your business up and running?

c.   Will you have enough finances to get the business started and maintain it for at least one to two years?

d.   Are you required to sign a personal agreement when signing a lease for your space, computers, or other equipment?

e.   Are you thinking of incorporating; you will need to open a new bank account after your incorporation is complete.

5. Decide the best way to promote your business

a.   What is the best way to promote your business?

b.   How soon should you begin an advertising campaign?

c.   Learn great ways to get referrals.

d.   How can you ensure sales?

e.   Try utilizing free advertising; have the local paper do a write-up of your business.

6. Be cheap; find ways to keep costs to a minimum

a.   Is it possible to start your business from home?

b.   Try to share your costs with another business until you are up and running.

   c. Get to know businesspeople in other fields—trading is a great cost saver.

   d. Used furniture and desks can reduce start-up costs dramatically.

   e. Make a list of all assets you will need and tell your friends— they may offer you items they have.

7. Develop an operating manual

   a. A simplified operating manual would be beneficial to your business success. Keep it simple, do not overwhelm yourself trying to be perfect, write one page at a time.

   b. Start with one page and write out some "rules" and slowly expand from there. Employees love to know the rules—a procedure manual provides just that.

8. Take care hiring employees

   a. Check references; check them all.

   b. Avoid hiring friends if possible.

   c. Create a list of questions that are important to your business and go through them all with each candidate. Write out the answers and compare all candidates.

   d. Call a second interview to double-check promptness, clothing style, cleanliness, and availability.

9. Honesty and Communication

   a. Stick to basic, governmental business rules.

   b. Make your own choices based on your personal morals.

   c. If you don't understand the rules, have someone teach them to you.

   d. Know that you are not the first person to seek honesty in business.

10. Pay attention to taxes

   a. Pay attention to taxes—they will not go away.

   b. Pamphlets and books on how to charge taxes for small businesses are usually free at your local tax office.

c. Consult a qualified accountant before starting up your business.

d. Learn what taxes you need to charge for your service or product and how to remit the taxes to the government.

4Gerber, Michael E. The E-MYTH REVISTED: New York, NY: HarperCollins Publishers Inc, 1995

REFERENCES AND BIBLIOGRAPHY

J.R. Tony Arnold, CFPIM, CIRM and Lloyd Clive, CFPIM. APICS - Supply Chain Management, The Educational Society for Resource Management. Falls Church, VA: 1995

Gerber, Michael E. The E-MYTH REVISTED: New York, NY: HarperCollins Publishers Inc, 1995

Small Business BC, 601 West Cordova Street, Vancouver, BC, V6B 1G1 Phone: 604-775-5525 In BC: 1-800- 667-2272 Fax: 604-775-5520 http://www.smallbusinessbc.ca Reviewed: October 2004

Vincent Peale, Norman, A Fawcett Columbine Book, Published by Ballantine Books, Copy write 1982 by Norman Vincent Peale

IDEAS AND PLANS

IDEAS AND PLANS

IDEAS AND PLANS

IDEAS AND PLANS

IDEAS AND PLANS

IDEAS AND PLANS

IDEAS AND PLANS

IDEAS AND PLANS

IDEAS AND PLANS

IDEAS AND PLANS

IDEAS AND PLANS